Time on the Grass

Bobby Robson

Time on the Grass

Arthur Barker Limited   London

A subsidiary of Weidenfeld (Publishers) Limited

ISBN 0 213 16845 6

Printed in Great Britain by
Fakenham Press Limited
Fakenham, Norfolk

Contents

I would like to thank everyone who helped me prepare this book, including Brian Scovell who wrote the words, Steve Dobell who edited it, my wife Elsie whose advice was invaluable, and my long-serving personal secretary Pat Godbold.

Bobby Robson   *May 1982*

Illustrations

The agony of waiting ... (Colorsport)
... and the joy and elation that success can bring! (Bob Thomas)
Returning to Southend Airport with the UEFA Cup
1981 UEFA Cup Squad (Bob Thomas)
With Patrick Cobbold and Ron Greenwood (Bob Thomas)
Playing in a charity match with Ron Atkinson and John Bond

Except where otherwise indicated, the photographs reproduced in this book were supplied by the author.

Introduction

by Brian Scovell of the *Daily Mail*

Bobby Robson is a man who is passionate about football. When he speaks about a player he admires, his eyes light up and his personality changes. He becomes animated and excited. He is talking about the game he loves and he wants to communicate that feeling to people around him.

This passion, which has been with him since his school days when he was a 'netty boy' playing street football at the backs of the terraced houses in Langley Park, a small mining village in County Durham, has helped him become one of the world's leading managers and coaches.

He has few interests outside football. The game consumes his energies, which are considerable, almost totally. He rarely allows himself a day off and if he goes on holiday he will usually watch a match or meet football people while he is away.

He comes from hardy coal mining stock and maintains that good health is one of the reasons for his success. His father Philip missed only one shift in fifty years down the pits, and his own record is similar.

He is at his desk before nine o'clock most mornings, and stays at the ground until early evening after taking the coaching. Several nights a week he is away watching football matches. His favourite television viewing is football, and his most enjoyable way of spending an evening is to witness a match in which his own team is not taking part.

When Ipswich are playing he is often so involved that he finds he cannot take any pleasure from it, unless the team hits a peak as it did once in St Etienne. This singular concentration on one small aspect of life, with its attendant pressures, would drive many men towards a nervous breakdown, but it leaves him untouched. He relishes the challenge. The telephone never stops ringing and his mail can average anything up to one hundred letters a day. He is constantly in demand.

His chief relaxation is to walk the family dog, Roger, a spaniel named after Roger Osborne, who scored the only goal for Ipswich in the 1978 FA Cup Final, around the farmland surrounding his beautiful country home, a converted farmhouse a few miles outside Ipswich.

It is a time when, away from the countless demands for his attention, he reflects on the problems of management. Every morning by eight o'clock he is out walking through the fields and woods, and again last thing at night. His other way of relaxing is to operate the motorised mower while cutting the two acres of grass at his property.

He admits to having no real hobbies outside his main one, football. He is a golfer but can't spare the time. He likes going to the theatre, only there are few evenings when he can fit it in. He reads, but only on long coach journeys or flights with the team. His wife Elsie, a former nurse who is now a primary school teacher, sees much less of him than the average wife; and so do his children, three sons who all went to public schools.

I first met him when he was a player with Fulham. He did some coaching for the Football Association at Paddington on a Preliminary Course – to make money to live, he now says – and it was apparent to all of us on that course that here was a man who was destined to become a manager of a Football League club.

His initial venture in management, with his first club Fulham, was ended abruptly when the financier Sir Eric Miller sacked him. Several years later Sir Eric, a friend of Sir Harold Wilson, committed suicide.

Though not a vengeful man, Bobby Robson made an appropriate comment. 'Shows how he stood up to pressure, didn't it?' he said. His dismissal, the 686th managerial sacking since the Second World War, left him determined to put himself in a position where no one could possibly sack him again.

He has achieved that at Ipswich, where he is the longest-serving manager in the country, an unbroken spell since January 1969. He found the players and built the club up himself. The board of directors, unique in British football because they are not power seekers, have let him do virtually as he liked.

He has been called a dictator but has shown that great power hasn't corrupted him. Now and again the friendly hand of either

John or Patrick Cobbold, his chairmen in his years at Portman Road, has restrained him from a certain course of action, as when he decided, wrongly as it transpired, that his career would benefit by joining the Spanish club Bilbao.

In his reign in East Anglia, Ipswich have finished in the top six no less than eight times. The season they struggled, when they finished eighteenth in 1977–8, they won the FA Cup.

In terms of consistency in one of the world's toughest Leagues, only Liverpool have surpassed this record in the same time – and they have been a rich, big city club. Bobby Robson has had to compete with the Liverpools and Manchester Uniteds with little money to spend and with an army of fans less than half the size of those of his rivals.

What money he has invested on his players, he has had to earn first. His management has been prudent and successful. Despite building two new stands and an indoor training area, Ipswich are financially sound, a rarity in English football. The club is a monument to what he has achieved.

Bromley, Kent
March 1982

One

A Survivor

My job can be simply defined. It is to win football matches. Up to the end of the 1981–82 season I had 330 wins, 245 losses and 184 draws as a manager, and that was sufficient to make me the longest-serving manager in the Football League.

In an occupation where the average length of time spent by a manager in his job was less than three years, I had survived at one club for thirteen years. There were nine occasions when I could have left to take offers from other clubs, but I refused them all. Some of the offers, like the £230,000 from Barcelona for a two-year contract, would have made me the highest paid coach in the history of British football.

I preferred to stay at Ipswich because I liked the working conditions, the directors let me do the job with little or no interference, and I liked the people and the place. I also felt happier working with players we had discovered ourselves rather than with million-pound players. Though Ipswich finished in the top six nine times in the past ten years, making them the second most consistent club in England next to Liverpool, I am aware that some people will say that I did not win the championship and therefore failed.

In the 1981–82 season we finished runners-up to Liverpool when I thought we were going to do it at last. The season before we came second to Aston Villa, and most people agreed that we were the best footballing side in Britain that year. We failed then because of having to play too many matches in too short a space of time. When I see what happened to Tottenham Hotspur in the final weeks of the 1981–82 season, I marvel that we finished as strongly as we did.

I was sure we had the best squad of players in the 1981–82 season, but we came second yet again because not all of them were fit to play at the same time. We hit the trip wire on 23 January in a fourth round FA Cup tie at Luton which we won 3–0. It was our ninth victory in succession and we were third in the table, two points ahead of Liverpool with two matches in hand.

In the second half Terry Butcher went to clear the ball with his head at the same time as Luton centre-forward Brian Stein swung his boot at the ball. Butcher is not a player who will pull back. He caught Stein's boot in the face and collapsed on the ground, blood pouring from his nose. After treatment, he carried on for a while but his nose kept bleeding and he had to come off.

It still wouldn't stop bleeding in the dressing-room afterwards and he had to be taken to hospital. That was the start of one of the most anxious periods of my life. Butcher, an England centre-half whom we had discovered ourselves and helped become an international player, became so ill in the ensuing days that he was literally fighting for his life. He needed countless blood transfusions. Thankfully, he recovered and nearly three months later was able to play again and regain his England place.

Losing Butcher was a blow to our championship aspirations, but in the same week we lost Paul Mariner, who needed an operation on his Achilles tendon, Frans Thijssen with a broken leg which was to restrict his senior appearances to a mere 17, and Russell Osman, who missed only two games before he was fit again.

These injuries came at the worst time of the season when we met Liverpool three times in a week. Ten days after the Luton game, we lost 0–2 at home to Liverpool in the first leg of the semi-final of the Football League Cup. Liverpool played exceptionally well that night, especially in the first half, and I remember looking at Craig Johnston on their bench and saying to myself that at £750,000 he cost more than the whole of my team.

If only I had £500,000 to spend on a player! The most I ever spent was £200,000 each on Kevin O'Callaghan, Thijssen and Mariner. Ipswich never spent more than that because the directors and I agreed that it was not worth putting the club at financial risk by speculating in the transfer market.

If Liverpool or Manchester United buy a million-pound player and they win matches, the gates will go up and they will recoup their outlay. But Ipswich average 22,000–24,000 each game whatever players they have and whichever position they occupy in the League. On the other hand, if Mark Lawrenson, the player I consider to be Liverpool's outstanding buy in the last year, had gone to Portman Road instead of Anfield, perhaps the title might have gone to East Anglia.

I regret not being able to boast a championship medal but I don't see it as a failure. My satisfaction at Ipswich has been producing good players and being happy in my work. When we lost a game the knives weren't out. My directors, some of them Old Etonians, still cling to what is now an old-fashioned view that you have to accept being beaten with good grace and that winning isn't everything.

More and more clubs are being 'rescued' by rich men who take over as chairmen and expect the manager to chase honours. These people know little about the running of professional football and I see their entry into the game as a disquieting feature. I worked for one once, Sir Eric Miller at Fulham, and I will never work for one again.

They appoint what I call box office managers, front-of-house people who talk well in public, and they expect instant success. I prefer the Ipswich way, which is a gradual evolution backed by financial prudence. We spend our money wisely, adding new stands, new facilities and developing young players.

I take great pride when I see players like Butcher and Osman playing for England and John Wark and Alan Brazil playing for Scotland. Most of our players have been groomed to international standard, and when I am asked what I have accomplished, that is what I point to – the players I have helped produce. Not many box office managers make players. They might buy some. They don't find them and coach them to stardom as I do.

It is virtually impossible to buy success in football. It comes through being patient and persevering in what you know is right. Happiness and job satisfaction is more important to me than being able to spend millions of pounds of someone else's money.

If there is such a thing as stability in football I think I have found it at Ipswich. The board of directors is the same as it was when I arrived in January 1969, except that one member has died. The other change is that Patrick Cobbold has succeeded his brother John as chairman. There was no coup when the takeover took place. John felt his brother ought to have a go at the job.

I have been supremely lucky in my career to work for the Cobbolds. They are priceless gentlemen, and are unique in football. The other four directors, Murray Sangster, Harold Smith, Willie Kerr and Ken Brightwell are in the same mould. Other clubs are sometimes taken over by rich men on ego trips who want to win trophies. Even the more established clubs go through upheavals if the team isn't winning. But at Ipswich we carry on the same way, building for the future and improving the ground as we go. When I first went to Portman Road I owed much to the then secretary Wally Gray who, unlike many club secretaries, was an independent man who supported the manager. He was not a directors' stooge as some secretaries are at other clubs.

To win football matches the manager has to do two things. First, he has to make money. In my time at Portman Road I sold forty-five players for £2,658,050 and bought fourteen players for £1,038,000 which gave me a profit of £1,620,050. So I have been successful on that count.

Second, he has to make players. In one match in the 1981–82 season nine of the players in my team had come up through the ranks. Ipswich are unusual in another way too: the club is not heavily in debt. The latest £1.4 m stand is being paid for as it goes up. Every season the club aims to balance the books, so that unlike many clubs we are not living beyond our means. The urge to be winners at all costs has plunged many clubs into serious financial difficulties.

Transfer fees in England are now the highest in the world, although income through the gate is less than the income at comparable clubs in other countries.

Tactically, the way the game has constricted, with the players finding less and less space to play in, has meant that goals are at a premium, so if a player proves he can score goals he is in demand and his price rockets upwards. English football is almost in the state the game was in Italy a few years ago when near-bankrupt clubs mortgaged their possessions to buy over-priced goal-scorers.

Transfers are conducted on hire purchase and some are paid for over as long as four years. It is a crazy situation, and when it is accompanied by a wage scale that clubs cannot afford, it becomes crazier still. After freedom of contract was introduced, players were able to hop from club to club if they chose to and insist on short-term contracts of one or two years which destabilised the buying club.

Handling contracts these days is a nightmare for a manager. Players hear what their colleagues are earning in another club and want the same. They decline to sign long-term contracts that give them and their club some security. More and more clubs hand the responsibility for negotiating contracts over to a managing director, a paid director or a financial director.

At Ipswich I do all this myself. The directors give me the authority to conduct the financial side and I must say it is one of the least enjoyable parts of my job. I am happiest when I am working with the players as a coach.

On the Continent running a football club is primarily the responsibility of two men, the technical director and the coach. I believe we are going the same way in this country. The complexities of the modern game are making it almost impossible for one man to perform both roles, as I do at Portman Road.

Although the transfer system has brought financial problems to many clubs I do not think it is necessary to ban transfers during the season, as has been suggested. All it needs is some sensible controls. For example, the Football League should insist that every transaction should be paid for within a year. That would cut fees considerably.

Where the system goes wrong is that clubs seeking glory plunge themselves into debts from which they cannot escape. Buying a new player now and again is, I believe, good for the game, just as it is good for a brewery to introduce a new beer or for a food company to produce a new line. It stimulates interest and excitement and helps sales. But doing it too often is financially reckless and ill-advised.

Being a football manager is a high pressure business. If the team loses, the manager is blamed, although often he is helpless to do anything about it. His life is dictated by what eleven men do on the football field. In my time in football the game has become much more competitive and demanding. The pressures on managers today are much greater than they were on Herbert Chapman, George Allison, Matt Busby, Stan Cullis and other great managers of the past. The media coverage is greater. Herbert Chapman wasn't being asked to appear live on television and on the radio. He didn't have mass press conferences after every match. Every decision he made wasn't analysed in great detail.

To stand up to these pressures the manager needs a strong constitution and good health. I cannot remember when I had the last day off because of illness. But the real pressure is mental, and I find that I have been able to withstand that just as well although I am a workaholic and have few interests outside of football.

After matches I rarely sleep well because, like the players, I play every game through, evaluating every move and analysing every mistake. As we usually play twice a week, that means I have two bad nights which I never make up. But I have never taken a sleeping tablet in my life. I don't believe in them. I don't take tablets of any kind.

The manager is carried along by his peaks and pulled down by his disappointments. The game attacks him and drains him but he has to put up with it and accept it. Firstly, he is fired by a love of the game. Bill Shankly, for example, had a passion for football which sustained him to the end of his life. How deep that feeling runs can determine how long the manager survives. By the time he is in his late forties, the manager is thinking of getting out.

I am not thinking that way myself. I feel I can carry on until I am fifty-five, or perhaps older as some Continental coaches do. There is a mistaken belief in English football that management is a young man's profession, that the man in charge has to wear a track-suit and should not be much older than the players. I believe in wearing a track-suit and being with the players but there is no substitute for experience.

To do the job my way, it is necessary to be a hard worker who puts his job before his family. Football becomes like a drug. I do not delegate much, not because I do not trust the rest of the staff but because I think I can do the job better myself. My coaching staff will assess players for me, but before I buy a player, I must see him several times myself. Any manager who buys a player without seeing him play is asking for trouble. But it does happen.

It is easy to sell good players, much harder to buy them. The worst time to buy is just before the deadline when the pressure is on clubs. The best time is when you don't need them, like in the close season when there is plenty of time for the new player to fit in.

Many clubs these days are run by partnerships. Brian Clough had Peter Taylor at Nottingham Forest and Terry Neill and Don How at Arsenal are just two that come to mind. I do not think having an assistant of this type is necessary. Often I think managers bring in a number two to give a friend a job. There is only one place where the buck should stop, and that is with the manager.

When I came to Ipswich Cyril Lea was the coach and I kept him on. Nowadays managers will bring in their own staff and the old staff will be sacked. That is not a good thing either. Cyril was very conscientious and loyal and when the fists were flying in the dressing-room early on in my managerial career, he was by my side. But after I turned down an offer from Barcelona I decided I wanted Bobby Ferguson as my chief coach because he was a fellow Geordie and I felt he was better for the job than Cyril. I hated doing it but it was necessary for the club. We compensated Cyril and he went to Stoke. Soon after he went to Hull to join Mike Smith, whom he had worked under with Wales.

Some managers prefer to pass on their coaching responsibilities to their assistant but I am not among them. When Justin Fashanu was banned soon after his arrival at Nottingham Forest, Brian Clough said Justin would have to work on improving his game out on the training pitch. If Fashanu had been my player, I would have been the person who straightened him out. At Forest, Clough leaves that to his coaches. A few years ago Ipswich were staying at the Dutch training centre in Zeist, Holland, and Derby County, then managed by Clough, were also staying there. Clough took the players on walks, but Jimmy Gordon did all the training.

I am a firm believer in the value of coaching. Good players can be made better players by practice and getting them to improve their skills. Jack Nicklaus didn't become the world's top golfer by just going out there and playing. Geoff Boycott made himself into the leading run-getter in the history of Test cricket by his dedication to practice. Whenever he thought he was developing bad habits, he went back to his old coach Johnny Lawrence. Most of what I achieved at Ipswich was down to coaching. When John Wark, Alan Brazil, Russell Osman, Terry Butcher and other young players arrived at Portman Road they weren't exceptional footballers. We made them into exceptional footballers.

I suppose to a certain degree I am a dictator at Ipswich, because I have overall power. I consult my staff but I do not necessarily agree with them. I make the final decision, and that is the way it should be, otherwise a football club soon falls apart. The board of directors must have ultimate power – I accept that – but if the job is being done properly there is no need for them to interfere.

Tommy Docherty once said in the High Court that managers had to be cheats and liars, and was expelled from the Football League Executive Staffs' Association for saying it. I do not agree with him. Bertie Mee was honest. Bill Nicholson was honest. And I like to think that I am honest with my players. There are times when a manager has to be discreet, but that doesn't mean he should tell lies. If I am asked a question I do not want to answer, I say I am not prepared to comment, or I fudge over the issue. When buying and selling players, managers obviously do not want the details to be revealed too soon, but they can be less than open without telling lies.

The manager who lies to his players is soon found out and the players lose all respect for him. An example of how being too honest can rebound was the Micky Mills affair late in 1981 when Sunderland manager Alan Durban, needing an experienced player to act as his coach, asked me if we were prepared to sell Mills. I could have agreed a price and got rid of Mills, as managers often get rid of players who are nearing the end of their careers. Or I could have kept the approach quiet and not told Mills.

Instead, I was frank with Mills and left a decision to him. If he thought he would better his career and profit from it by accepting the Sunderland offer, then I was prepared to let him go. But I preferred him to stay with Ipswich. Somehow, it came out that I was trying to sell my most experienced player and that made me angry. Mills has been a very loyal servant to Ipswich over the years, and I would never kick him out.

Managers sell players mainly for business reasons, the way Brian Clough sold Trevor Francis to Manchester City. That is why managers rarely socialise with players or become too friendly with them. I like to think I get on well with all my players at Ipswich, but I have never had them to my home or socialised at their homes.

I cannot afford to have favourites. They are all equal and demanding of my attention. They call me 'boss' as they called Bill McGarry 'boss' before me. No one, not even Mills, calls me by my first name. Discipline is one aspect of professional football that hasn't changed much since I came into it. Players who break the rules are fined in a way that would probably cause a walk-out in a factory or office. But this military-style discipline is very necessary, otherwise the system would break down. Players are always ready to test the manager and get away with things. But they respect firmness and fairness. The manager who fails to uphold strict discipline is soon found out and removed from his job.

It is easy enough for a manager to be sacked for any number of reasons, but these days player power can be disruptive and a weak manager soon becomes a statistic on the dole queue. There are some unbelievably bad appointments made by clubs. Directors rarely examine all the credentials of a potential manager before deciding whether he is the right man for their club. Often someone recommends a candidate and he is appointed on the flimsiest of grounds. Naturally enough he fails, and the cycle starts again.

I would like to see a voluntary system adopted by the clubs whereby they agree not to appoint a new manager unless they give him a three-year contract. Three years is the minimum time for a new man to make his mark. Anything less than that is unfair on him and the club. Such a limitation would make directors think harder before confirming their new manager. The trial and error manager would disappear.

I remember the late Alan Ball senior once telling me what his chairman said to him when he was appointed manager of Preston North End. Posing for a photographer, the chairman put his arm round Alan and said: 'We sink or swim together.' Two years later, Alan was called in to see the board and knew in advance that they were going to sack him. He asked: 'How many of you are going to sink with me?' Of course none of them did. Directors, I feel, should be more accountable for their mistakes.

Football is now dominated by publicity about its financial problems, and most of those problems have been self-inflicted. Clubs that cannot afford to pay players £800 a week or more, whatever the average is for top players in the First Division, have been doing it because they feel they must compete with the Manchester Uniteds and Liverpools.

Paying players exorbitant wages can be counter-productive and I believe this is being seen in the area of coaching. When I was a player, I earned twenty pounds for some years, and to improve my financial position I worked as a part-time coach at schools and colleges, earning an extra five pounds or so a week. Today's players earn so much that they don't have to do that, and therefore few of them have coaching experience when they decide they want to become managers.

The man who persuaded, almost insisted, that I should become a coach was Walter Winterbottom, the first manager of England after the Second World War. Walter was a brilliant coach and a first-class mind. England's decline in world football accelerated the day the Football Association decided they no longer wanted him. When he resigned as manager, the post of secretary fell vacant and he applied for it. Instead, the FA appointed Sir Denis Follows, a very capable and able administrator but a man who lacked the football knowledge and experience of Winterbottom.

If Walter had become secretary, I am confident our standing in world football would be much higher today. What a great partnership he could have had with Sir Alf Ramsey. How well he would have worked with Ron Greenwood! There are few great minds in British football, yet we felt we could afford to discard someone like Walter. It was a tragedy.

During the sixties and seventies, England's international standing diminished while the domestic game continued to remain strong, competitive and attractive to the people who went to watch it. Much of the credit for maintaining the Football League as one of the world's best Leagues went to Alan Hardaker, a powerful, single-minded man who ran it almost like a dictator.

But while the League ploughed on, the international side suffered, and Alf Ramsey and Don Revie were broken by the conflict between the two. The League is important, but our international rating depends on what the England side does, and over the years we neglected it. It always struck me as being lunacy that the League did not allow the England manager to have his players for a week before vital matches. Other countries do it, but not England. Ramsey and Revie had to work with patched-up squads and players who were less than fully fit or exhausted after punishing League matches. Training was frequently a joke. And afterwards, when the players should be together to talk over what went wrong and work on tactics, the squad would disperse back to their clubs, usually on the same night, driving home through the early hours and adding to their tiredness. What a way to run a national side!

The manager would say: 'Bye lads, see you in three months' time!' There were no regular training sessions, no detailed planning. The odds were always against Ramsey, Revie and Greenwood, and it was a miracle we managed to qualify for the 1982 World Cup.

We had a great start winning the World Cup in 1966 but we let it slide. The FA finished up paying a considerable sum in Corporation Tax which sickened everyone in the game. I don't think Walter Winterbottom would have let that happen. Alf Ramsey received a bonus of a mere £5,000. Our priorities were woefully wrong then and things have not improved much. There is a lot of pressure being England manager, and who wants that for a salary below that of the top club managers? Much re-organisation still needs to be done.

After Hardaker died, the League started to decline as the country went into recession and clubs had to find other ways of raising money. Soon some were receiving more from their commercial activities than they were through the gate, but that cannot last. The end product, the football team, must be the prime consideration.

All kinds of innovations were talked about, among them ground sharing, merging of clubs and artificial pitches. It is inevitable that there will be some natural wastage with the League being reduced from its ninety-two clubs, and once the First Division is cut to eighteen clubs, I feel many of the problems will disappear. Playing six less matches a season will lose each club £300,000 a year and that money will have to be made up from other sources such as sponsorship of the League championship and Football League Cup, now the Milk Cup, and television and the pools.

A smaller First Division comparable to the leading Leagues on the Continent will enable the England team to have more time together and give the England manager a better chance of being successful. Clubs merging or sharing grounds are merely delaying the inevitable and I do not support either idea. Neither do I agree with artificial pitches which some chairmen are advocating on the grounds that these pitches will enable clubs to diversify and earn income from other sources such as pop concerts.

The breakneck speed of our game is not suited to artificial pitches and anyone who has seen football played on unnatural surfaces in America knows how boring the game is on an artificial pitch. The ball is continually in the air bouncing over the players heads and out of play. Terry Venables has done a fine public relations job for QPR's artificial pitch, but having seen my reserve players struggle to keep their feet on it, I refuse to believe it has a future.

Crowds want to see goals and excitement, and everyone in the game should remember his obligations to the entertainment side of the game. In this respect, the introduction of three points for a win has been a sound innovation which has resulted in more teams being prepared to attack away from home.

I also feel those of us in the professional game need to work harder. On most afternoons football clubs are deserted. Players should be back there in the afternoons practising like a Nicklaus or a Boycott. Until this kind of dedication is seen again in English football I feel we will continue to struggle at the very highest level.

Two

Early Days

If it is true that a man's early upbringing and environment help make him what he is, then it's no surprise that I have never been afraid of hard work. I came from coal-mining stock in County Durham in the North-East, and my father, Philip, now seventy-eight, missed only one shift in fifty-one years down the pit.

He started work the day after he left school at the age of fourteen and retired at the age of sixty-five. I remember seeing him go off to work when he was suffering from 'flu or with boils. In those days, if you didn't work, you weren't paid. If you failed to turn up, someone else was waiting to take your place.

My father is a remarkable man. My earliest memories of him are of seeing him come home from work and strip off in front of the fire in the kitchen to have a bath. As in every mining cottage of that time, we didn't have a bathroom. Our bath was a tin one which was kept fastened outside the house on the outhouse door. It was a laborious process filling up the copper next to the fire – the same fire that heated the oven – boiling the water and then transferring it to the bath on the kitchen floor.

Friday night was the family bath night and we would use the same water. My father would lift us out and my mother would dry us. It was a custom that never changed. There were seven of us: my father, my mother Lillian, who is now seventy-four, and five boys, Tom, who was born in 1925, Philip, born in 1929, Ronald, 1931, Robert William, 1933, and Keith, 1939. My mother wanted a girl, and when she was expecting Keith just before the outbreak of the Second World War, she was sure her wish would be fulfilled. But it wasn't to be. She never showed her disappointment.

In that part of the world, people accepted what they were given without complaint. We were a happy family and I can't remember having fights with my brothers. What we had, which wasn't a lot, we shared. Sport was our outlet – football in the winter and cricket in the summer.

We lived in a four roomed, terraced house, two bedrooms upstairs and a sitting-room and a kitchen downstairs. There was a small yard at the back and at the end of it was the outside toilet and coalhouse. There was no lighting or heating in the toilet. We had to take a torch or a candle with us when it was dark. Often in the winter it would be frozen up and my father had to mend burst pipes.

My father did all the jobs around the house, the plumbing, the painting and decorating, and he repaired our shoes for us. That was another family task – he would take out his iron last and sit hammering in the nails which he used to hold between his lips. Once I remember he was stitching some leather when the device he was using went through one of his fingers. It had a hook on it, like a fishing hook, and he couldn't get it out. He went next door to show his neighbour.

The neighbour, Jack, told him to hold his hand while he yanked the hook away, ripping off a lump of flesh. Next day he was at work as usual, but it took some time for the wound to heal. He never complained. He was strict and when he thought it was necessary he would give us a crack round the ear. There was an occasion when I was nine when I stayed out late at a travelling fair which visited our village. He told me to be back at eight, and when I hadn't returned, he came looking for me. I spotted him and ran home. When he arrived he gave me an almighty spanking with his belt.

On Sundays we used to go to the Methodist chapel. My parents were Methodists and we had to go to Sunday School. The highlight of the week was the walk we used to go on after chapel on Sunday, up the New Road towards the hills and the fresh air, away from the grime of the coal mine which dominated the village.

It always finished the same way, with my father buying us a twopenny cornet each. That was our treat. Like most other children in the village, we wore 'handed down' clothes. There was no shame in that. Few families could afford to buy new clothes. They had to make do with what they had and sew up the holes and tears. My parents did all they could for us. They did a smashing job.

My mother was a typical wife of those times. She was always at home to do the domestic chores and bring up a big family. She was the daughter of a miner and was brought up from the age of four by her grandmother after her father died. She is a lovely woman, though not as outward going as my father. A few years ago they had the telephone installed. She still takes a long time to answer it.

She will sit there and say to my father: 'You answer it.' She still has the suspicion of the telephone that many old people have who lived most of their lives without it. They think a telephone call means that something bad has happened, that there is a crisis.

I was born on 18 February 1933 in a terraced mining cottage at Sacriston, a small village of about three thousand inhabitants. All five sons in the family were born at home. In those days few births took place in hospitals. A few months after I was born, we moved to a similar house in Langley Park, another mining community a few miles away. My mother and father still live in Langley Park, in another terraced house which they have occupied for thirty-five years and rented from the National Coal Board. A few years ago they bought it from the Coal Board for £2,500.

When I was fourteen months I was lucky not to have been killed in an accident outside the house. A deliveryman in a lorry was visiting the houses with lemonade, Stones ginger wine, 'Tizer' and the other soft drinks which were our weekly drinks order, and unbeknown to my mother, I toddled out of the door when she wasn't looking and started to pass in front of the lorry.

The driver didn't see me as he got back in the cab and started up the engine to drive further up the road. The front wheel, or the front of the lorry, caught me on the neck and knocked me down. For some reason which he didn't know himself, the driver suddenly pulled up. He couldn't have seen me.

Everyone gathered round, fearing the worst. My arm was stiff and my mother tells me she had to cut the material off my jacket to get it off to examine me. Apparently my only injury was bad bruising of the neck, although I did have an abscess on the face later which was thought to be a side effect.

Although our house was small I can't remember any fights with my brothers. Four of us used to sleep in one bedroom in two double beds. We always found time to study and do our homework. Tom, the oldest, left school at fourteen and went to work as an apprentice engineer in the mine. He attended night school and qualified for his present job, chief engineer to one of the Coal Board's biggest regions.

Philip, second oldest, started life as a bricklayer, qualified to become a master builder at night school and ran his own business before selling up and buying two newsagents' shops. Phil was blown up while serving with the British Army in Korea and that caused a lot of anxiety in the family at the time. My mother nearly collapsed when the telegram arrived from the War Office. Happily, he made a complete recovery.

Ron, the third in line, had the best education of all of us. He went to grammar school, matriculated and became secretary to the colliery manager. He would say to us: 'One day I'm going to own my own shop and I'll make a fortune.'

After working for a while at the NCB head office in London's Victoria, he returned to Langley Park and bought a provision shop which he has now turned into a supermarket. Keith, the youngest, took a correspondence course and later gained a Bachelor of Arts degree through the Open University. He became a senior draughtsman with Mobil Oil and now travels all over the world designing oil rigs.

I, too, went to night school, after leaving school at the age of fifteen. I took a job as an apprentice electrician at the colliery, checking faulty motors, coal cutters and other items of equipment. I earned four pounds ten shillings in my first week, and had to get up before six in the morning to clock in at 6.50.

There was never any fear that I would work for the rest of my life in the pits. When the teacher at Langley Park Infants School set the class an essay on 'What I would like to do for a career', I wrote about the imagined delights of being a professional footballer. I kicked my way through more pairs of shoes than any boy in that school. We were the 'netty' boys, the street footballers. 'The netties' were the toilets at the end of the yards which backed on to the concrete street. We used the wall for heading practice. I had two particularly close friends, Jimmy Cooke and Jackie Ellison, and we used to chalk goals on the walls and play heading games across the street.

We would throw the tennis ball up with one hand and try to head a goal across the other side of the road, a few yards away. For goals we used to stick a couple of tin cans down about thirty yards apart and play six-a-side matches. Many times I kicked the kerb and came home with bruised toes, hardly able to walk. My father just had to be one of the best cobblers around to keep me in shoes! If someone kicked the ball on a coalhouse roof, we had to climb up and retrieve it. When I was nine years old I fell about six feet to the ground, breaking an arm.

Despite spending most òf my time out of school hours kicking and heading battered old tennis balls, I was fairly bright at junior school and it came as a surprise when I failed my eleven plus exam. Instead of following Ron to Durham Grammar School, I had to attend Waterhouses Modern Intermediate School three miles away, where the headmaster wasn't too keen on football. He refused to let the school enter the local league and the only organised football I played between the ages of eleven and fifteen was the occasional friendly match arranged by the PE teacher.

I think this lack of competitive play early in my career helped me, because I spent more time working on skills. That is where so many youngsters fall down today: they are thrust into competitive games at too early an age before they have had a chance to pick up basic skills.

Four of the young boys from our area went on to play football professionally – George Johnston, who played for Lincoln, Dickie Brankston, who also played for Lincoln, Leo Dale, who signed for Doncaster, and myself. We used to think it was Utopia – football in the winter, cricket in the summer and marbles when we had time to play. I was a good marbles player! As for cricket, I couldn't bowl, but was a fair batsman. After I joined Fulham, I used to come home in the close season to play for the local cricket club.

My formative years came in the War. My father didn't serve in the Forces because he was a miner, and the labour force at the pit was swelled by the Bevin Boys, teenagers who failed the Army medical but were deemed fit to dig coal. My father was a teetotaller and a non-smoker and he wouldn't let his sons drink or smoke in the house. He wouldn't let us bring girlfriends home either until we were working. Besides mending our shoes, he would also cut our hair. That was another family tradition. He would sit us down in the chair, put a sheet round us, and out would come the scissors.

With the money he had saved and scraped together, he would take us to Newcastle, seventeen miles away, for home games at St James's Park. We were often the first people in the queue at 12.30, and sometimes he would treat us and buy unreserved seats.

I can remember Len Shackleton's first game. It was against Newport County and Newcastle won 13–0. They were all heroes to me – Albert Stubbins, the centre-forward, Jackie Milburn, 'Wor Jackie', Alf McMichael, Charlie Wayman and Bob Cowell.

The first organised football I played was after I left school, for a team called Langley Park Juniors, an Under-18 side. A committee was formed in the village to run it and we had some good results against local youth sides, so good in fact that scouts from the professional clubs came to watch us and I found myself in demand.

Three

Fulham for the First Time

Whenever a boy comes to Ipswich for a trial, I make a point of seeing him myself and showing him around. I do this because I know how hurtful it is to be invited to a club and virtually ignored. It happened to me at two clubs at the start of my professional career. The clubs were Middlesbrough and Southampton.

I was fifteen and a half when I was asked along to Ayresome Park for a trial. David Jack was the manager, but I never saw him. I thought I did quite well but never heard again from them. By this time scouts were turning up regularly at our games, and after a cup-tie I was approached by Bill Rochford, who was then playing for Southampton. Bill was a Mick Mills figure at the Dell in those days, a very respected senior player.

'I think you have a good chance of becoming a pro,' he said. 'Would you like to come to Southampton if I can fix it?' Southampton were in the Second Division but that didn't worry me. It was the big opportunity. No more having to get up before six o'clock in the morning!

I spent a month at the Dell and played in the 'A' team along with Leo Dale, my village friend, who was a winger of the old-fashioned type. Leo had the talent to have played for England but was keener on greyhound racing than football, or so it appeared. He was always at the race tracks.

Ted Bates, later manager and now a director of Southampton, was still a player then, and there were some other fine players on the staff like Don Roper, who went to Arsenal, and Jack Edwards and Bill Ellerington, who was to take Rochford's place. Sid Cann had just taken over as manager, replacing Bill Dodgin senior, who went to Fulham. I never saw Sid, and when my month was up I went home to Langley Park without having been made an offer.

Clubs couldn't sign youngsters until they were seventeen, and when I attained my seventeenth birthday in 1950 I suddenly found myself in demand. Newcastle, Middlesbrough, Southampton, Lincoln, York, Blackpool, Huddersfield and Fulham all wanted me. I had my pick. As a Newcastle fan, I suppose I should have taken their offer, but they were the big spending club in those days and few local players made it to the first team. They signed so many expensive players from other parts that youngsters were discouraged from signing.

After their earlier indifference, Middlesbrough now offered me four pounds a week in the season and three pounds a week in the close season. Bill Rochford was so upset at the way Southampton had treated me that he advised me to take Fulham's offer. He knew Bill Dodgin well, having played under him, and said he would look after me. Fulham's offer was seven pounds and six pounds, the maximum offer in those days. They had just been promoted and had several players whose names were known to me like Archie Macaulay, Bobby Brennan, Eddie and Reg Lowe and Ian Black.

My parents were apprehensive about me going to live in London at so young an age but agreed I could go providing I kept up my apprenticeship as an electrical engineer in case I failed to make the grade in football. Fulham found me digs in Inglethorpe Road, one of those streets of terraced, Victorian houses near Craven Cottage, and I took a job with a company in Victoria that had a contract to carry out work on the Festival of Britain site and later, the Festival Hall. I started work at seven in the morning and was only able to train on Tuesday and Thursday evenings.

I was so tired after matches in the reserve side that one day Bill Dodgin, a kindly, considerate man, said: 'You have to make up your mind what you are going to be, an electrician or a footballer. You can't be both.' I was also continuing my studies at night school and obviously I had to give something up. After talking it over with my parents, I decided to sign full-time as a footballer.

Fulham was a happy club in the early fifties – from the chairman, Tommy Trinder, down to the apprentices – and even relegation in 1952 didn't change the mood. I felt in awe of Tommy Trinder. He was the first comedian I had met. He drove a blue Rolls-Royce, and it was the first Rolls I'd ever seen.

It was there I met my best friend, Tom Wilson, who is now chairman of a big firm of estate agents. Tom was a good player, a right-back, and was known by everyone as 'Whipper'. This was because when he was standing in the goal area for corners or free kicks, his arm would flick out behind him as though he was whipping a horse in the final furlong. He never knew he did it and couldn't understand how the habit had developed, because he had never ridden a horse. Another player I was close to at the time was Bill Dodgin junior, Bill senior's son. We grew up together and completed our footballing educations at the same time. Some Sundays Bill invited me to the family home at Worcester Park to listen to his music. We remain good friends.

Johnny Haynes was an office boy when I joined. He was seven months younger than me and clearly destined for a great future in the game. In seven years as an England player, he gained fifty-six caps. It should have been more really. He was an outstanding passer of the ball, probably one of the best passers we have had in this country.

Off the field, you couldn't meet a nicer fellow, but on it he was narky and always moaning. He was such a perfectionist that it irritated him when the deficiencies of players around him caused a move to break down. Though he was in his teens when he first came into Fulham's League side, the senior players accepted his criticisms without argument. They knew he was a better player. One of the butts of his frequent tirades was 'Tosh' Chamberlain, the club's left-winger, and there was that celebrated occasion when Haynes found him with a brilliant long pass over the full-back's head only to see Tosh let the ball run out of play.

'You stupid ——— ————', screamed Haynes. The referee raced up to John and took his book out to caution him. 'Hey,' said Tosh, 'you can't do that. He's my mate. And I am a stupid, ——— ————.' Tosh wasn't a bad player. He could beat an opponent, had considerable pace and was capable of striking the ball exceptionally hard with his left foot. But he didn't like being knocked about.

I doubt whether there has ever been a more humorous man in professional football than Tosh. Almost everything he did could provoke a laugh. In one game he disappeared for a while, and when he re-appeared, someone asked him where he had been. 'I went to the toilet,' he said.

From the time he made his début for England Schools in a 6–2 victory over Scotland, Johnny Haynes was destined for greatness. He was a spontaneous, instinctive player with a built-in football brain. But he wasn't idle with it, as some gifted players can be when it has all come easy to them. No one worked harder in training than he did. He was superbly fit.

It must have come as a considerable surprise to the man in the street in 1951 when John failed his medical for National Service. I failed mine as well, and if it had happened today there would have been a national outcry. How could two very fit sportsmen be exempted? Was it a fiddle? John was exempted because hc had suffered from perforated ear drums, and the Army were cautious about ears because of the risk of further damage that might occur when guns and rifles were being fired close by.

Just before I was due to attend the Medical Board at Croydon, Frank Osborne, Fulham's general manager who virtually ran the club for many years, called me in and said: 'Any chance of you failing? Have you ever had anything wrong with you? Eyes, ears?' I said I had suffered from mastoids some time previously, and his eyes lit up. He had me examined by the doctor, who said there was a possibility I might get away with it.

The club doctor wrote to the family doctor in Langley Park and I took the report on my ear trouble with me when I attended my medical at Croydon. I was graded C3, which meant I wasn't required to join up. Some of the other Fulham players like Roy Dwight and Bill Dodgin were less fortunate, and there was a lot of mickey-taking when I arrived back at Craven Cottage. I was christened 'Cloth Ears', and it was a name that stuck for some months.

Fulham had not long been promoted the year I arrived, and although several experienced players were signed we were relegated along with Huddersfield in 1951–2 with only twenty-seven points. I cannot recall that altering things much at the club. It was still half a social club, half a football club. In the next four seasons I was there, we scored more than two goals a game in the Second Division but only occupied a mid-table position. In season 1953–4 our goal tally was 98 for and 85 against, which is an indication of how generous we were in defence. Crowds of between twenty and twenty-five thousand continued to roll up. Charles Dean, the Victorian-style old gentleman who was at one time chairman, used to let Frank Osborne and Bill Dodgin get on with it, and the other directors were equally sincere and genuine people – men like Chappie D'Amato and Jack Walsh, who lived next door to the ground.

Several of us used to come back for training voluntarily in the afternoons. That was where I learned the game. Bill senior believed in constant repetition of skills. There wasn't as much coaching as there is today, nor as much tactical thinking. But we used to enjoy what we were doing. Upstairs at the Cottage was one of the most heavily used snooker tables in London. It was a very relaxed club with an easy-going atmosphere.

Frank Osborne rarely saw a game through to its conclusion. He would sit in his seat at the start and always find some excuse to get back to his office. He was one of the most superstitious people I have met in the game, and football is well known for its superstitious people.

On one occasion he was scouting at a match in Glasgow when he decided to leave at half-time as the player he had come to watch wasn't as good as he had been told. His early departure meant he had two hours to wait for the London express train, so he dived into a barber's shop for a trim. As he was sitting there, 'Sports Report' came on the radio and the announcer read out: 'Birmingham City 0, Fulham 2.'

Fulham weren't in the habit of winning many away matches that season, and to encourage it to happen again, Frank went through exactly the same routine a fortnight later. He went to Glasgow, watched half a game, left to go to the same barber's shop and caught the same train. He must have done that two or three times before accepting that it wasn't the magic formula to guarantee Fulham away points!

I made my debut for Fulham in March 1951, just after my eighteenth birthday. The game ended in a 2–2 draw at Sheffield Wednesday and I remember how tired I was in the second half. There were no substitutes in those days, otherwise I think I would have come off.

One of the highlights of my first stay with Fulham was a tour we made to Canada and America by boat and train. It lasted six weeks and I enjoyed every minute. The Atlantic was at its roughest when we made the outward sailing, and I was the only player who wasn't sick. We travelled across North America in luxury, eating sumptuous meals on trains and sleeping in comfortable berths. It was far more relaxing than today's footballing trips.

While we were in Victoria Island, British Columbia, we were presented with hand-carved totem souvenirs, and Frank Osborne was given a large one which was to go on display in the club boardroom.

When we had a bad spell the following season, he decided that the totem was putting a curse on the team and one day decided to do something about it. He went to the boardroom, seized the totem, took it to the boiler room and threw it in the fire!

Charlie Mitten, who later became the manager of Newcastle, was one of the characters in the Fulham side of that era. Charlie was a big man in those days. He had not long returned from Bogota with Neil Franklin, where he had gone to earn big money. Fulham signed him from Manchester United for £20,000, which was a substantial fee. Charlie was very smart and dapper and knew where to find things on the cheap that the rest of us might want. One day he came in and said: 'Right, now, which ones of you want a new rain coat? I've just got a supply of cloth and can get it made up for you.' He went round measuring us ... but we never got our rain coats!

On another occasion, Johnny Haynes and I were having some treatment when Charlie came in carrying a black greyhound. 'Come on, Haynesey,' he said. 'Get off that table. The dog has a sore fetlock and needs some heat on it.' Johnny Haynes was only a teenager, like me, and he dutifully made way for the dog. Frank Penn, the trainer, strapped on the equipment and gave the animal some short wave. It had a muzzle on, as I recall, because it was a bit of a snapper.

One of the nicest, most genuine players on the staff was the right-back Robin Lawler, an Irishman who couldn't stand the sight of blood. During a game at Everton, Gordon Brice, our centre-half, received a nasty cut across his forehead when Dave Hickson, the Everton centre-forward, brought his head back suddenly and butted him. The players gathered round as the blood poured from Gordon's head.

Eddie Lowe, another of Fulham's characters, started looking on the ground as though he was trying to find a contact lense. 'What are you looking for?' asked Robin.

'It's his eye,' said Eddie. 'One of his eyes has fallen out.' Robin nearly fainted! After Ian Black left Craven Cottage one of the youngsters on the staff, Tony Macedo, was promoted to the first team. Tony was a rather flash guy who was always throwing himself about spectacularly and bouncing the ball in an extravagant manner. He was a brilliant keeper, however. In training he perfected the art of bouncing a ball in each hand on the ground, swapping over hands and even doing it behind his back. The Harlem

Globetrotters were in London around this time and I think they had a great influence on him.

In one match against Spurs he was doing his Harlem Globetrotter act, pretending to throw the ball to Jimmy Greaves when the ball slipped out of his hand and rolled towards Jimmy. It finished up in the back of the net, as you would expect with Jimmy around. Macedo was mortified, and what Johnny Haynes said to him was unrepeatable.

There were some interesting people on the Fulham staff in the early fifties, players like Joe Bacuzzi, Len Quested, who went to Australia, Tony Barton, now manager of Aston Villa, Roy Dwight, who broke his leg in an FA Cup Final, Jim Taylor, a fine centre-half, Reg and Eddie Lowe, Bedford Jezzard, whose record of 154 goals for the club between 1948 and 1956 still stands, and Jimmy Bowie.

The club used to go regularly to Worthing for golfing breaks, and Bowie, a single handicap man, was always challenging the rest of us to play for money. At dinner one night in Worthing we concocted a plot to ensure that he lost his money. He persuaded Robin Lawler, who wasn't much of a golfer and who didn't own a set of clubs, to take him on for ten pounds, Robin having the appropriate shots for his handicap.

The plan was to let Robin hit off the tee and for the rest of us to go round with him, supposedly to advise him. Arthur Harrison, the club professional, came round with us, and wherever Robin's ball landed up, we would gather round in a tight circle so that Jimmy Bowie couldn't see, and Arthur would whip a club out of Robin's bag and play the shot. Robin would spray the ball off the fairway but invariably seemed to reach the green with a better score than Jimmy.

And just to make sure that Jimmy struggled, we had Frank Osborne up ahead to tread on Jimmy's ball if it was in a good lie. Jimmy couldn't understand it and never twigged what was happening. He had given us odds of 3–1 against Robin and had to pay up at the end of the round.

Jimmy Hill was one of the prime movers behind getting us down to Worthing. He would say to Frank Osborne: 'The lads are looking jaded, Frank. They need a bit of a break and some fresh air.' Off we would go, especially if a cup-tie was coming up. Jimmy Hill came from Brentford roughly at the same time as Ron Greenwood. He was an inside-forward and Ron was a centre-half.

Jimmy was a non-stop grafter, medium skilled and a terrific enthusiast. He never stopped talking. He was always demanding the ball, and with Johnny Haynes doing the same, there was often a conflict of views. When George Cohen first came into the side, a wag shouted out: 'Cohen, when the Rabbi calls for the ball, give it to him.' Jimmy was known as 'The Rabbi' because of his beard, which hasn't changed over the years, except maybe in colour.

He liked to push himself forward, and his enthusiasm for the game was communicated to the rest of the staff. One of Walter Winterbottom's Full Badge FA Coaches, he always had ideas about improving our training methods.

I played one season with him before my departure to WBA and enjoyed the experience. Jimmy has a dominating personality and a persuasive manner. It was at this time that I became interested in coaching and went on courses myself. Jimmy Hill and Ron Greenwood were good men to be with at this stage in my career.

Ron was different to Jimmy. He was a deep thinker, and when he said something, it commanded respect. Whereas most of us would stay on after training, some to play snooker, he would go straight home to Uxbridge where he lived at the time. He was a family man first.

Ron gained one England 'B' cap, against Holland in 1959. He was a sturdy player, not exciting to watch but effective and hard tackling. Though not tall, he attacked the ball in the air and was a good jumper. He was a very purposeful player and played the game simply, knowing his own limitations. Both men were obvious managerial material, and it was no surprise to any of us when they were successful as managers.

Bobby Keetch was one of the youngsters, and he eventually took over the centre-half position in the first team. Keetchy was a very hard player but he could play a bit too. He was very good in the air. He always seemed to have a beautiful girl with him. For a while he had an affair with a titled lady who used to lend him her Alfa Romeo. It had a turntable to play records on, which at that time was looked on as a pretty sophisticated piece of equipment to have in a car. I used to share a room with Keetchy, and one day the rich lady rang and he amazed me with the ripeness of his language. 'She loves it,' he explained.

We used to call Jim Langley 'Gentleman Jim'. He was given the name because whenever he sent an opponent flying, he would always pick him up, say sorry and brush him down. I can't remember him ever being booked. He taught me a lot about whacking opponents and letting them know you are there. He had an immense throw and would preface it by an elaborate winding-up gesture with his hands, a kind of warning system which alerted defenders as much as his own players!

One of his predecessors at full-back was a hard player Fulham bought from Arsenal, John Chenhall, who was known as 'Chopper'. John was a bit of a womaniser and regularly attended the Hammersmith Palais. One night he was trying to impress a girl and said: 'I'm Chenhall from the Arsenal.' The girl replied: 'I'm sorry, I don't go to speedway.'

Fulham used the WM formation which was in vogue at that time, and usually played two wingers at the same time, Arthur Stevens or Johnny Campbell on the right and Tosh on the left. Johnny was signed from Belfast Celtic. He was a sprinter and a statistics man. He loved boxing, and if a fighter was knocked out, he would pull out his stop-watch and say: 'That was two minutes, thirty-five seconds into the round.' Or if a goal was scored, he would say: 'He was twenty-three yards, nine inches from goal.' Sadly, he contacted peritonitis and died.

In those days I was played as an attacking inside-forward alongside Beddy Jezzard, performing the kind of role that Alan Brazil or Garry Birtles carries out today. I didn't have Jimmy Greaves's eye for goal but I managed to score 132 goals in my career, which, considering I moved back into midfield after eight years as an attacker, wasn't a bad record.

Beddy was a very popular player at Craven Cottage. I still see him sometimes. He hasn't changed. He was a bustling type of player, difficult to shake off the ball. We were all delighted when he was picked to play for England against Hungary in 1954, the return match after England's cataclysmic 6–3 defeat at Wembley the previous year. As it turned out, it would have been better had his début been delayed, because England were trounced in Budapest 7–1. Ivor Broadis came into the dressing-room, took off his boots and said: 'Don't touch them. They're red hot after chasing around after that lot.'

The 6–3 defeat at Wembley revolutionised English football. Previously we had been cocky and insular. We had produced good individual players like Matthews, Finney, Mortensen, Ramsey and little Ernie Taylor, and we thought the supply would be endless. But in tactics, techniques and team play we lagged behind other countries. Not enough thinking and planning went into our football.

Before the Hungarians arrived, you would rarely see more than two or three balls in use at training grounds. At Fulham, for example, if you asked a certain coach for a ball, he would say: 'What do you want a ball for? You get one on Saturdays!' The emphasis was on physical work. To have a ball per man, as the Hungarians did, was unheard of, but that changed rapidly.

I was at Wembley that day in November 1953. A coach left Craven Cottage at 11 a.m. and we were all excited at the prospect of seeing the unbeaten Hungarians. We knew little about their players, but their record seemed to suggest that they were something out of the ordinary. They might give us a game, we said. England were unbeaten at Wembley, and though no one expected the citadel to fall, we suspected the Hungarians might offer a similar kind of challenge to the Rest of the World side which drew 4–4 at Wembley the previous month.

Before the game the Hungarians came out to warm up, and around us people were saying: 'They'll be knackered before the game.' Sides never warmed up in those days. They just went out and played. When the match kicked off, it was obvious that England were going to be thrashed. The Hungarians used a new system which hadn't been tried here, 4–2–4, and their centre-forward Nandor Hidegkuti, played in a deep position some thirty yards off his centre-half. Poor Harry Johnston, England's centre-half, didn't know who to mark. It was the end of the WM formation. In future England played with two centre-halves, one marking and the other spare. No longer was a single centre-half capable of dealing with continental attacks, not when they played 4–2–4.

The vision of players like Bozsik was outstandingly good, and the mastery of the ball exhibited by Puskas, in particular, was superior to anything we had seen in English football. But the most impressive feature was their teamwork. Whereas England worked in triangles, the Hungarians had every player involved in the team unit. Seeing England ripped apart that day had a profound effect on me. I decided that my education was a long way from being completed. Soon afterwards, I started attending FA coaching courses at Paddington Street, off Baker Street, along with Ron Greenwood, the late Jimmy Clarkson and Jackie Goodwin, stalwarts of the scheme started by Walter Winterbottom.

For too long English football had drifted along in a complacent daze, not expecting other countries to catch up, or as had clearly happened, overtake it. Up to then, Winterbottom, as England team manager, had little say in team selections. He was handed a list of names by the International Committee, amateurs who had never played the game themselves. They made sure that their own clubs had a representative in the side. For example, it always appeared odd to me that such a fine player as Ray Barlow of West Bromwich Albion only received one cap, while Jimmy Dickinson, a good player but not quite as good as Barlow, received forty-eight caps.

After 1953, the FA allowed Walter to make recommendations about selections. But the team was still picked by the Committee!

Four

West Bromwich Albion

Vic Buckingham was one of the best talkers I have met in the game, and when, in March 1956, he asked me to sign for his club, West Bromwich Albion, I thought it was the natural thing to do. I had never played on the Albion ground, the Hawthorns. Nor had I been to West Bromwich.

If I had had prior warning, I wouldn't have signed. After living near the River Thames in London, moving to the Black Country was like going down a coal mine. I had just married Elsie, who came from Langley Park and was a nurse at St Stephen's Hospital. We lived in a flat off Wandsworth Bridge Road and were very happy. I caught a bus every morning to Fulham and she caught a bus in the other direction to the hospital.

So why did I leave? I still don't know. Fulham were still in the Second Division, but I loved playing for them and there was no pressure from the directors, the fans or anyone else. I suppose it started with the sacking of Bill Dodgin senior. He was a nice man and it upset the players to see him go. His successor was Dugald Livingstone, a dour Scot. Soon after he took over Livingstone called me in and said the club was short of money, and as West Bromwich Albion, a successful First Division club, had offered £25,000 for me, he was prepared to let me go.

A transfer fee of £25,000 was big money in those days. The record stood at £34,000, which Sheffield Wednesday had paid to Notts County for Jackie Sewell in 1951. Trevor Ford, Danny Blanchflower (both £30,000) and Tommy Taylor (£29,999) were the only other players to have cost more than that in 1956. I wondered why Fulham were short of money. A club's outlay in those days was much less than it is today. Players were on a maximum wage – Haynes still had five years to go before he became the first £100-a-week footballer – and the amount spent on insurance, ground improvements and general upkeep was proportionately much less than the sums paid out today. In addition, attendances were much higher. But somehow, the money had disappeared.

I caught a train to the Midlands on the Friday and signed the same day. Vic Buckingham didn't show me any houses and my wife wasn't invited along, as happens in today's transfers. The club booked me into a small hotel and next day I made my début against Manchester City at home. We lost 4–0, and it was one of the unhappiest occasions of my life. Manchester City had copied the Hungarians and were using the deep-lying centre-forward plan. Bobby Johnstone, the Scots international, Ken Barnes, father of Peter Barnes of Leeds, and Don Revie were key figures in the side. As for me, I hardly got a kick.

Albion won the FA Cup in 1954, but they had an old side, with players like Ronnie Allen, Ray Barlow, Jim Dugdale and Johnny Nicholls – good players, but players who were ageing. Vic Buckingham did his best to cheer me up but it was several months before I began to settle down. After training the other players would rush off and I was left on my own. I had never felt so lonely. Ray Barlow helped me while away the time in his digs near the ground and in a cafe, but it wasn't until I became friendly with Don Howe that I started to like my work.

As for fixing me up with a house, the club couldn't manage that. They arranged for Elsie and me to hire a couple of rooms in someone else's house! Vic Buckingham was a suave, colourfully dressed man who always had a hankerchief drooping from his lapel pocket. He had a habit of clearing his voice loudly as he spoke, and it was a sound I was to get used to over the next few years because his team talks were longer than those of any manager I have ever encountered.

The average time of a Vic Buckingham team talk was about an hour. His record was two hours. No one dared fall asleep or let his attention wander. Vic was very strict and commanded the respect of his players. He had coached Ajax, the Dutch club, and was one of the few English coaches with foreign experience. He was also an intelligent person and sometimes would use French idioms in his team talks. None of us knew what he was saying, but we were pretty good at pretending.

He used to say: 'I don't want you to go out there and go lah-da-lah-da-lah and then bonk! I want you to go out there and go lah – da – lah – da – lah – da – lah – da – lah and *then* bonk! At the end of his oration, he asked for questions. I was new to this, and at my first team talk Ray Barlow said: 'If he asks for questions, don't say a word. If you do, I'll fill you in. He'll talk for another hour.' Not surprisingly, there were never any questions.

I was sorry when Buckingham left the club in 1959. He had been a great benefit to my career, and was an articulate and romantic individual. By then I had settled down and was enjoying playing for one of the best footballing sides in the country. It was a good time to be a player. Teams used to attack each other, and there weren't eighteen players in a confined space as there often is in modern football. Albion were one of several teams who had copied the Hungarians and were playing 4–2–4 with only two men in midfield. It was a much more open game than today's.

Vic left soon after we returned from a tour of Canada in the summer of 1959. He was cited in a divorce action and was sacked shortly afterwards. Albion's directors were honourable, strait-laced Victorian gentlemen who didn't like scandal. They met regularly, every Tuesday, and their prime aim was to keep the club solvent.

The Canadian tour was a leisurely affair – six weeks on transatlantic liners and trains – and it was newsworthy because Maurice Setters, Albion's England Under 23 wing half, was sent home because of his behaviour. Maurice was a funny lad. The club employed a photographer, Albert Wilkes, to take the pre-season team picture, and one year Maurice asked him to do three passport photos for him.

Albert duly took the pictures and later sent him a bill for half a crown. Maurice refused to pay. 'He comes here and takes my picture and sells it, why should I pay him?' he said. Albert sent another bill. Again Maurice ignored it. Finally, Albert asked the club for the money and they paid. When it was time for the next club photograph to be taken, Maurice declined to sit with the rest of us. Vic Buckingham was very angry. 'Get in that picture,' he said.

'Not if he's going to take it,' Maurice replied. 'Right, in my office,' shouted Buckingham. They went into Vic's office, and when they returned Setters posed with the other players. But as Albert stuck his head under the hood to take the flash picture, Setters turned his head the other way, and the club photo went out that year with one player's face not showing!

On the field, Maurice was a hard player, a good tackler but a player who could be ruthless with it and show his studs. He was a fit lad and had good balance. He was a player you would rather play with than against. He had a bad relationship with the club's trainer, Dick Graham, the former Albion goalkeeper who later became manager of Crystal Palace and Colchester United.

I liked Dick, although some of the other players resented his methods. He believed in working players hard, and his values were right. But he could be authoritarian, and when Setters came in for training in the morning he would give Dick the Nazi salute and say: 'Heil Hitler!'

As we stood on the upper deck waving with the other passengers to the people on Liverpool Dock at the start of our trip to Canada, he said to Dick: 'Listen you, you watch yourself on this boat because the first chance I get, you are going to be overboard.' The players forgot all about it until the fifth day of the voyage when Buckingham decided to end the socialising and start some training. Although it was a holiday, we were supposed to be playing some matches. The captain of the ship allowed us to use the First Class 'A' deck and after some warming-up exercises under Dick Graham's direction, Dick produced a new ball for a five-a-side.

I was standing next to Ronnie Allen, who was a keen betting man. 'I'll give you six to four that the first time the ball goes to Setters, he'll kick it into the sea,' he said. He was right. Setters booted the ball over the railings and within seconds it was half a mile away as the vessel steamed on. Dick Graham was extremely angry. 'I might have known a fellow like you would do that,' he said.

On the final night before landing the purser arranged a Carnival night and invited us to take part in a fancy dress song contest. Only Setters took up the invitation. He came on, contestant number 9, wearing only a jockstrap and two halves of a coconut strung across his chest. He carried a wet fish in his hand and sang 'Body and Soul'. At first sight we felt like disappearing under the table. The jockstrap did not conceal much. But the rest of the passengers thought he was very funny and gave him an enthusiastic reception.

Wherever we went in Canada, Setters had to be different to everyone else. At a reception in Toronto he turned up in a red dickie bow tie when we were all wearing the offical team tie. 'Take that off and put your tie on,' said Buckingham. Setters refused. But after further remonstrations from the manager, he turned up in brown trousers when the team wore grey.

The incident which decided Buckingham to take disciplinary action happened on a long night flight from New York to Edmonton. I was sitting in a window seat next to Setters, and Buckingham sat across the aisle in the same row. We were dozing off – it was a four-engined propellor-driven plane which took nearly twice as long to do the flight as modern jets – when I noticed Setters taking out his sick bag and blow into it.

When it was full of air, he banged it with his other hand and the loud bang woke the other passengers, some of whom panicked. Buckingham said: 'Why don't you grow up?' Setters answered: 'Why don't you belt up?' It was obvious that no manager could allow a player to continue behaving like this, and when we arrived in Vancouver, the furthest point West on our trip, Buckingham ordered Setters to return home on his own. Not long afterwards, he was sold to Manchester United for £30,000.

He was one of a number of players Matt Busby bought as he strove to rebuild his side after the Munich air crash in 1958. I remember being at home and hearing the news of the disaster on the radio. It was one of the greatest tragedies in the nation's sporting history. Busby was well on his way to producing one of the finest club sides we have ever had. Some of our most promising players died, including Duncan Edwards, a cocky player of immense strength, Eddie Colman, Roger Byrne and Tommy Taylor.

Busby was a great man, a nice man. He was an excellent judge of a player and when he had the players he wanted, would tell them: 'Go out and play.' He wasn't a tactician or a man who believed in long team talks. He was a man who encouraged and inspired. Albion drew the rebuilt United side in the sixth round of the FA Cup in that fateful 1957–8 season, and it was an occasion I will never forget. We drew 3–3 at home against Nottingham Forest in the third round and in the return match lost Setters through injury when the score was 1–1 after twenty minutes. Amazingly, we came back and won 5–1!

When we drew 2–2 at home against Manchester United we thought a similar miracle might happen. Mass hysteria seemed to have overtaken the city of Manchester. It took us much longer than usual to reach Old Trafford through the milling crowds and we learned that twenty thousand people were locked out. Inside the ground, sixty thousand people were willing United to victory, and we lost 1–0. The following Saturday we were back at Old Trafford in a League match, and in a different atmosphere we won 4–0.

I was so short of money in my early days at WBA that I used to walk to the Hawthorns from my home at Handsworth. I earned extra cash coaching at schools and for a while worked as a £2-an-afternoon representative for the Bromford Iron and Steel Company, later switching to the Sandwell Engineering Company.

I bought my first car in 1958, the year I made my début for England. It was a second-hand Morris Minor and I paid two hundred pounds for it. I bought my first house at the same time for £2,425, putting down a deposit of £525 and borrowing the rest. We'd saved every pound we could. Bert Millichip, the present WBA chairman and chairman of the Football Association, was the solicitor who did the conveyancing on our house.

Ronnie Allen was probably the most influential player in the Albion side in the fifties. Ray Barlow, who was not far behind him, called him 'The Little Caesar' because he had this confident, leadership air about him. He did a lot for me. He sharpened my footballing brain and made me a better player. He had a great touch and was a fine volleyer and goal-scorer. Ronnie was a withdrawn centre-forward of the Hidegkuti–Revie–Bobby Johnstone mould and I'm sure he made Derek Kevan and Johnny Nicholls into England players. One season Kevan, Allen and I shared seventy-seven goals. In modern football, it is exceptional if a whole team scores seventy-seven goals. I scored twenty-eight of them from midfield.

We played with two wingers, Frank Griffin on the right and George Lee on the left. Most sides had two wingers. It was the era of Stan Matthews and Tom Finney and every kid in the country wanted to be a Matthews or a Finney. Nowadays kids want to be strikers or midfield players. No one wants to be a winger because they are not in the game enough.

To be a winger, a player needs patience and discipline. Most players can't be patient. They are looking for work, drifting inside and seeking the ball. The modern player is taught to get involved in the game. If a move breaks down, he is expected to become a defender and compete to win the ball back again. This utilisation of players' abilities has worked against wingers.

You wouldn't see Stan Matthews chasing back after opposing players. His job was to get the ball, beat opponents and put over crosses which led to goals. In 33 years, he played in 886 matches, including 54 internationals, 701 League games and 86 FA Cup ties, and he scored 95 goals, although he never had a reputation of being a goal-scorer. He retired a week after his fiftieth birthday and now says he retired too early! He was a fantastic player, a unique performer whose arts and crafts will probably never be seen again.

The breed was dying out when Alf Ramsey took over the England side in the sixties, and despite having three wingers in his World Cup squad – Terry Paine, Ian Callaghan and John Connelly – Alf preferred to have four workers in midfield in Alan Ball, Nobby Stiles, Martin Peters and Bobby Charlton. He won the World Cup and almost every manager in the country copied his 4–4–2 system. The Hungarians' 4–2–4 was out. The new system might have gained results, but it certainly wasn't as exciting to watch.

One of the few contemporary players who has been successful as an orthodox winger is John Robertson of Nottingham Forest. He has been the one outstanding winger at club level. Peter Barnes and Laurie Cunningham have been too inconsistent, Steve Coppell does a good job without possessing the real surge and wizardry on the ball that is needed, and Ipswich's Kevin O'Callaghan is only just starting his career.

One of the most skilled players in my time at the Hawthorns was David Burnside, who lived near me and became a family friend. Elsie, my wife, is Godmother to his first child. He always carried a tennis ball in his pocket, and as he walked to the ground he would kick it against walls to help improve his technique. No one does that now. I don't know why not, because I cannot think of a better way of improving skill. Burnside became so proficient with the ball that he could keep a football in the air for longer than anyone I had ever seen without letting it hit the ground.

We once asked him how many touches he needed for his personal best. 'I don't know, over a thousand,' he said. Keeping the ball up is relatively simple to a skilled professional footballer, but the secret is concentration. It is easy to get tired and make a mistake.

David used to make sure that the ball sometimes rested on the back of his neck, or shoulder, to give him a few seconds' rest. Once, when we played a Russian team at the Hawthorns, he was asked to perform his repertoire of tricks on television – and was paid a fee of fifty pounds. That set the other players moaning. 'We're getting four pounds for playing ninety minutes, and he's getting fifty pounds for seven minutes of tricks,' one of them said. We beat the Russians 6–3 in a marvellous match that was a reciprocal visit after Albion's tour of Russia the previous season.

The food was so bad in Russia that most of us existed on lemon tea and ice cream. Most players were ill but we still achieved some creditable results, beating the Red Army side 4–2, drawing in Leningrad and beating Tbilisi 3–0. When foreign clubs visit Russia they don't play ordinary clubs. They play the best. So to go there and come home unbeaten reflected great credit on Albion. It was after that tour that Dick Graham introduced fruit into the dressing-room. There was always a bowl of apples, oranges and fresh fruit available, and he also had some flowers on show.

One day Wilf Carter pointed at the oranges and said to Burnside: 'I bet you couldn't juggle one of those.' Burnside said he could, and when Wilf threw a Jaffa at him, he caught it on his foot and flicked it up in the air. Dick Graham was a stern character in training, with his US Marine-style crew-cut, but he had a sense of humour and he brought in a wastepaper bin.

'Here, see what you can do with this,' he said. Burnside duly caught the waste bin on his foot as it was tossed across the dressing-room. After that, we always had a waste bin in the dressing-room. We also had a radio and music. Dick was full of ideas about calming nerves before matches and making the dressing-room a more restful place. I thought they were good ideas. He was a man who was attempting to bring the game forward.

The Albion players used to make a habit of betting on trivial events, and one of the prime initiators was Barry Hughes, whose antics in a televised Dutch match a few years ago made him a national celebrity in Britain. Barry was mainly a reserve at the Hawthorns, and to augment his £12-a-week wages he would point to a vase of flowers at lunch and say: 'How much would you give me if I ate all those flowers?' The rest of the players would have a whip round and perhaps raise a pound and he would proceed to eat the flowers!

Another of his 'acts' was to drink a colossal number of glasses of water after training – he couldn't afford more expensive liquids! One day he drank sixteen glasses in succession to earn himself another pay-out.

West Bromwich Albion faced fierce competition from Wolves around this time, as well as from Aston Villa. Wolves won the championship three times in that decade – 1954, 1958 and 1959 – and only missed the Double by one point in 1960. The Midlands set the pace and the rest followed. Wolves pioneered night football in those historic matches against Honved, Spartak and Real Madrid, and the other clubs copied them.

Wolves were exponents of the long-ball game, and if three out of five passes found their target, which was usually centre-forward Roy Swinbourne or, later, Ted Farmer, they were content. In some ways the game hasn't changed. The early pass from the back to the front men, bypassing midfield, is still the prime ball providing it is success-ful. Nowadays players are more bunched and there is less space, so there is more danger of giving the ball away.

With defenders of the quality of Ron Flowers, Billy Wright, Eddie Clamp, Bill Slater and Bill Shorthouse, and with Malcolm Finlayson in goal, Wolves were a hard team to play against. And they had two outstanding wingers in Johnny Hancocks and Jimmy Mullen, who were later replaced by Harry Hooper and Norman Deeley.

Though the emphasis was on the long ball, Wolves had fine midfield players in Peter Broadbent and Colin Booth – although Booth, a brilliant player in training matches, rarely reproduced his best form in the League. Overlording Molineux was Stan Cullis, one of this country's greatest managers. Stan was a stern taskmaster, but I find that players would rather work for a man like that than one who is too easy-going. Players don't like it if a club lacks discipline and organisation.

They might moan about discipline, but they prefer that to chaos. Stan writes to me occasionally and has given me useful advice in my career. Over the years a number of other clubs have tried to prise me away from Portman Road, but Stan once counselled: 'If you have a good board of directors, stick to them like glue.'

Stan was at Molineux thirty years, sixteen of them as manager, and it was a surprise when he was dismissed in 1964 with a year of his contract remaining. John Ireland, the then Wolves chairman, ended that unique thirty-year association with a statement of just twenty-eight words – roughly one word per year.

Wolves were succeeded as England's leading club by Spurs, whose manager Bill Nicholson was similar in many ways to Cullis – hard-working, disciplined and a good judge of players.

Football is about pairs, and Spurs had some exceptional pairings in their Double-winning side – Danny Blanchflower and Dave Mackay, Bobby Smith and Jimmy Greaves, and Terry Medwin and Cliff Jones. Nicholson shortened the game by reviving the short pass. It was exciting to watch. He was a gruff man and didn't bestow praise lightly, but knew what he wanted. He made some brilliant signings. Probably the best of all was Dave Mackay from Hearts for £30,000. Dave was an inspiration to everyone around him.

At the Hawthorns, Gordon Clarke had succeeded Buckingham but stayed in the job only a short time. Gordon was a nice, gentle man who was more suited to the Number Two role. Within a year he was to hand over to Archie Macaulay, a Scots wing-half who played for Brentford and Arsenal and managed Norwich City during their FA Cup run in 1959 when, as a Third Division club, they reached the semi-final.

Archie was a good tactician. He had the capacity to spot what was going wrong and do something about it, but we rarely saw him. He was known as 'The Scarlet Pimpernel', and the players would come in during the morning and ask: 'Has anyone seen Scarlet?' He was often late for training and usually left before the end.

There was one occasion, before a match at Ipswich in my final season, when he failed to turn up in time to join the coach as it left on its seven-hour journey to East Anglia. This was before the M1 was fully opened, and we used to go down the A34 through Stratford. But this time we headed in the opposite direction – towards Sutton Coldfield. The coach drove into a housing estate and stopped outside Archie's house to pick him up.

We set off southwards and Archie's wife drove his car behind the coach. After a while, Archie got off and joined his wife. We didn't see him that night at the hotel, nor at the ground when we arrived. At two o'clock Don Howe and I decided we would have to take charge in the dressing-room. I was the club captain, and Don the senior pro.

At 2.20 Archie walked in and said a few words. He stayed only a short time and after the match, which we lost 3–0, we saw him only fleetingly. Apparently he was spending a weekend with friends in Norwich.

That was the season Ipswich won the League title under Alf Ramsey. It was a remarkable achievement. They had no dynamic players, no internationals. In fact, they had some quite ordinary players. Roy Bailey, father of Gary Bailey, was not a great goalkeeper, and some of his defenders were unlikely to command big fees in the transfer market. Their success was a tribute to Alf's ability to get the best out of players. They had a simple understanding and exploited a basic method of playing. Jimmy Leadbetter played as a withdrawn winger on the left, hoping to pull the right-back out of position for Ray Crawford and Ted Phillips to use the space.

Crawford had a fine goal sense, and Phillips possessed a lethal shot. For a short spell they were the unrivalled marksmen of English football. On the right, Roy Stephenson played as an orthodox winger, supplying crosses to the strikers, and at the back Andy Nelson and John Elsworthy were reliable defenders.

I was still at WBA when our first child, Paul, was born in 1957, followed by Andrew in 1959. Our third son, Mark, was born at Epsom in 1963, and with a growing family, I felt I needed an increase in wages. Jimmy Hill, who was chairman of the Professional Footballers' Association, won the fight with the Football League to remove the maximum wage in 1961, and from then on it was up to players to negotiate their own wages. In the early negotiations between the PFA and the League, the PFA only wanted an increase in the maximum, but the League refused to agree and there were plans by the players to strike.

A few years earlier, in 1957, the intervention of the WBA players into PFA affairs had not had an auspicious start. Jimmy Guthrie, the Scot who captained Portsmouth in the 'monkey gland' FA Cup Final in 1939, was surprisingly sacked as chairman at the annual meeting on a motion put by Len Quested, the former Fulham and Huddersfield player. It was said that the rules prohibited Guthrie from holding office, although he had been at the centre of the PFA's fight to win some kind of freedom from the bosses.

The Albion players thought this was unfair and wrote protesting about his dismissal. Cliff Lloyd, the secretary, wrote back and said we had no right to express an opinion in the matter because our membership had been lapsed for two years. We hadn't paid our subscriptions. This came as a surprise to us because we had been handing our dues to a collector.

Apparently the collector hadn't handed them over! The club came to our rescue and paid off the arrears and deducted the money so much a week from the collector's wages. When Fulham chairman Tommy Trinder decided to pay Johnny Haynes one hundred pounds a week in 1961, any idea that the clubs would get together and impose a uniform pay scale evaporated. It was then up to each player to get as much as he could, and to each club to work out its own pay arrangements.

It was the start of bonuses and incentives. Eric Taylor, the late general manager of Sheffield Wednesday, introduced a crowd bonus – which was a sensible idea at the time. Other clubs preferred position bonuses. At the Hawthorns the directors decided to pay the senior players twenty-five pounds a week plus five pounds appearance money. I would be earning thirty pounds a week while Johnny Haynes, whom I partnered in the England team at the time, was earning one hundred pounds a week.

As club captain, I went to see Jim Gaunt, the chairman, and said: 'If I'm getting this, the others can't be getting much.' Mr Gaunt was a man who could be fixed in his ideas. He couldn't see the strength of my argument, and after a further meeting following the World Cup in Chile, I told him it would be best if I left the club. I was happy at Albion, but with a wife and two children to support, thirty pounds a week wasn't enough. Don Howe and Derek Kevan, fellow England internationals, were offered the same. Don was also unhappy but, having lived in Wolverhampton all his life, was unwilling to move.

In August 1962 I was removed from the captaincy, and Don Howe took over. 'This will enable him to settle down and play football,' said Archie Macaulay. There was no chance of that. I was determined to go unless the directors increased my wages. Again they refused to compromise, and I was put on the list.

Fulham, who inquired about me the previous March, immediately offered £20,000 and their bid was accepted. They were willing to pay me forty-five pounds a week, less than half what Haynes was receiving but fifteen pounds more than what Albion were offering. I agreed to rejoin Fulham, providing Albion paid me the £580 accrued share of benefit that was owing. The League refused to let Albion pay it, and the dispute dragged on nearly two years before I half won my case and was paid £280 in benefit. The remaining £300, which should have been my share of the transfer fee, was withheld.

I sometimes think of my own dealings as a player with clubs over wages when I see my own players to talk about contracts. Many clubs have a financial director or a general manager to deal with contracts. At Liverpool, for example, Peter Robinson performs this role.

But at Ipswich the directors let me do all the haggling with players. I have a budget each year and I know I have to work within that budget. The reason why so many clubs are in trouble financially is that they are paying their players too much money, more money than they are taking through the gate. No company can afford to do that for too long without going bankrupt. In a football club, it puts a strain on the commercial side of the club to raise extra money to bridge the gap. In an era of recession it is not easy to bring in money.

I do not blame players for seeking as much money as they can get, but they can only be paid what the club can afford. That is the rule I have always followed at Ipswich. In the 1980–1 season the average basic wage for a top First Division player was little over £500 a week. I did not think that was excessive, providing the club had attendances to sustain a wage bill of around £750,000.

A tricky area is when a manager is dealing with older players. Most players expect to continue to receive increases even though they may have passed their peak. It is hard to persuade an older player to accept that he should be earning less, rather than more. Things have changed since I was a player. Nowadays a large proportion of a player's income is invested in a pension fund which can be repayable when he is thirty-five.

Five

Playing for England

When I first played for England, against France on 27 November 1957, there was no club versus country controversy as there is now. Wolverhampton Wanderers, who won the League Championship that season, played only forty-six competitive matches, forty-two in the League and four in the FA Cup. That is nearly fifty per cent less than Ipswich played in the 1980–1 season.

There was no League Cup, or Milk Cup, as it is now. English club sides had not begun to take part in European competitions, and the British Championship was played during the season – not at the end when players were tired. Walter Winterbottom, the England manager, could have his choice of the best players in the country, though even he did not really have an unfettered choice, because the FA's International Committee still selected the team after he made his recommendations.

What I am saying is that the odds weren't stacked against England as they are now. Yet we were still unable to make a major impact in the World Cup in 1958 and 1962. Our football was more geared to the domestic side, even in those days, than the international side. Walter Winterbottom was one of the best talkers about the game I have come across, a rational, lucid man who put his ideas over with enthusiasm and style.

But then, as now, insufficient time was spent preparing the international side. Walter was a good administrator as well as an outstanding coach, and applied to succeed Sir Stanley Rous as secretary of the Football Association. He lost out to Sir Denis Follows and in 1963 quit football altogether to join the Sports Council. He was a sad loss to the game. Few people in Britain have influenced it more.

I was paid a twenty-pound match fee for my first international appearance, which was roughly one week's wages, and if you take a line through present-day rewards, the modern England player is underpaid when he receives his £100. Even when you take into consideration that the 1982 player can receive a bonus of £200 for winning and £100 for drawing, he is still underpaid. I believe the same feeling exists today as it did in my era: that the honour of playing for England is the main spur, not money. One change, however, is that today's players can share in the commercial perks that come from being a squad member. There were no perks in 1957!

The 4–0 defeat of France – I scored two of the goals and Tommy Taylor the other two – was the last time the Manchester United trio of Roger Byrne, Duncan Edwards and Taylor played for their country. Before England took the field again, the Manchester United air crash had robbed us of three very fine players.

All three were approaching their peak. Byrne was an intelligent defender, very quick and courageous. Edwards was a colossus, one of the finest players this country has produced. Kevin Beattie was on the way to rivalling him until injury, ironically sustained while coming on as a substitute for England, started to slow him down. Tommy Taylor was a marvellous header of the ball. There is no one better in the modern game. Only Paul Mariner can match him, and then only on a very good day.

England were still using the WM formation in 1957, with Tom Finney and Bryan Douglas on the wings and Ron Clayton and Johnny Haynes in midfield. Duncan Edwards used to alternate between playing at the back and in midfield. I was nervous in the coach driving to the match and asked Finney what it would be like. He was a nice, reassuring man.

'You'll find it harder than League football,' he said. 'Much harder. In the League you've got three or four to worry about. At this level, it's the whole lot. They're all good players. Steel yourself.'

I agree with those experts, including Bill Shankly, who say that Finney was England's finest ever all-round player. He had an excellent football brain, was very skilful, used space brilliantly, could score goals with either foot and could tackle like a defender. On top of all that, he was very brave and would go in where it hurt.

I was a reserve when the next England match was played, against Scotland at Hampden Park the following April. Jim Langley, my former clubmate from Fulham, replaced Byrne, and Bill Slater and Derek Kevan filled the holes left by the deaths of Edwards and Tommy Taylor. Once again we won 4–0 with Bobby Charlton scoring from one of the finest volleys ever seen at Hampden.

I was chosen for the close season tour to Yugoslavia and the USSR which was to precede the World Cup Finals in Sweden in June, and was restored to the eleven for the game in Moscow which ended in a 1–1 draw. Tommy Banks, a real character, was preferred to Langley. Banksie slowed down every winger he played against, sometimes with tackles that went beyond the limits of fair play.

Brian Clough went on that trip but failed to win a cap. He was much the same as he is today, a man on his own. But Cloughie was a prodigious goal-scorer in League football and deserved more than the two caps he eventually gained in 1960.

Instead, Winterbottom kept faith with my WBA colleague Derek Kevan. It was a controversial choice because, at the highest level, Kevan lacked skill. He was built like a tank and turned like one. But if he was facing the right way as the ball came to him, he was a handful for any defender, a powerful, aggressive player who scored some good goals. He was very similar in style to the Swede, Gunnar Nordahl.

I valued him at the time because he gave Albion qualities that were needed. But it was essential that he played in the right unit. At the Hawthorns he had Ronnie Allen and myself to complement him and he was at his best in that situation.

The game in Moscow was the first time England had ever played in Russia and the players all wished it was the last. Moscow was a sombre, grey place and the people viewed you with suspicion. The food was so bad we couldn't eat it, and when WBA toured there a year later, I made sure the club brought plenty of chocolate, cereals and other foodstuffs.

After a few days back in England, we flew to Gothenburg for our World Cup group matches against the USSR, Brazil and Austria. We were expected to go through to the quarter-finals with Brazil, but after drawing with the USSR 2–2, 0–0 with Brazil and 2–2 with Austria, we went out 1–0 to Brazil in a play-off. For some reason the FA decided to take only twenty players, not the customary twenty-two, and Stanley Matthews and Nat Lofthouse were left behind.

Billy Wright, the England captain, was not his usual, calm, composed self. The Press had revealed that he was to marry one of the Beverley Sisters and he was annoyed at the publicity. Bill was more of a physical player than a technician and he led by example. I liked him as a man. He was always keen to help young players.

In the match against the USSR, Finney drove the ball in from the wing and as Yashin dived at Kevan's feet, the ball ran out to me and I 'scored'. Istvan Zolt, the famous Hungarian referee, blew up for a foul by Kevan. I also 'scored' in the 2–2 draw against Austria but the goal was disallowed for off-side. If either of those two 'goals' had counted, England, not the USSR, would have gone through.

The 1958 World Cup saw Pele unveiled by the Brazilians. Only seventeen, he came in with Garrincha against the USSR, and the Russians were routed although the score was only 2–0. Without Pele, the Brazilians had failed to score against England's defensive system in our second match but I doubt whether that would have been the case had Pele and Garrincha been playing.

I was left out of the play-off match against the USSR and Peter Broadbent, the skilful Wolves inside-forward, took my place. I was not to play again for nearly two years, and in that time England's own teenage prodigy, Jimmy Greaves, had emerged to take the Number 8 shirt. By that time I had switched from being an attacking inside-forward to wing-half. Vic Buckingham asked me to make the change because Ray Barlow had been moved back to central defence and he needed someone to fill his creative role in midfield. I liked it. I found it easier than playing in attack.

My comeback game for England was a friendly against Spain in Madrid on 15 May 1960. I took over the Number 4 shirt from Ron Clayton and we lost 3–0. We were beaten 2–0 in Budapest a week later but most of the side remained when the Spaniards played the return game at Wembley on 26 October of the same year. This was one of England's most impressive performances of the sixties. On a saturated, heavy pitch, England won 4–2 with Greaves and his Tottenham Hotspur partner Bobby Smith scoring three of the goals.

Spain had some marvellous players at that time, including Luis Suarez, di Stefano, Francisco Gento and Del Sol, yet England gave them a lesson. Near the end we passed the ball around among ourselves to the 'olés' of a delighted crowd. It was the first time an England team had done that.

Bobby Smith was, despite his reputation, a very likeable man with a ready wit and quick smile. He would bet on anything. He was the ideal foil to Greaves. The goals kept flowing – 5–1 against Wales, 9–3 against Scotland at Wembley and 8–0 against Mexico. But Smith failed to stay in the side and his place was filled first by Gerry Hitchens and then by Burnley's Ray Pointer.

Hitchens, similar in style to Smith in many ways, scored twice in the 3–2 win over Italy in Rome in May 1961. I marked Enrique

Omar Sivori, the Argentinian and Italian international who was Europe's Footballer of the Year at the time. Sivori, who played with John Charles for Juventus and was Italy's highest paid player, was a very nasty customer. He played with his socks round his ankles and was a master at backheeling opponents, elbowing them and butting them with his head.

I managed to survive my ninety minutes with him – only to be dropped for the second match of the tour in Vienna. Walter Winterbottom wanted to see what Brian Miller of Burnley could do in midfield, so I was left out. I was back for the next four internationals, missed the return against Austria at Wembley and played what was to be my twentieth and last international game on 9 May 1962, the 3–1 victory over Switzerland at Wembley.

I went to Chile for the World Cup Finals that year but never played. Stan Anderson and I were the first choice midfield players in England's 4–2–4 system and Bobby Moore, then twenty-one, was a late call-up as first reserve. As it turned out, Moore played in all four matches and Anderson and I didn't play a single game between us.

Moore was obviously going to be a good player. He had a sound footballing brain even at that age and seemed a nice, earnest young man who was prepared to listen and learn. He was used in midfield but didn't have the pace to stay there. It was only a matter of time before he switched to his best position in the back four.

We stayed up in the mountains in a tiny mining village named Coya. A railcar had to be used to get up there, and we had to walk across a bridge to reach the dining hall from the small, individual homes we were billeted out in. From the viewpoint of seclusion and being able to work uninterrupted, it was ideal. But the facilities were so spartan that I cannot see present-day players putting up with them. Every day Harold Shepherdson, the England trainer, gave us a huge tablet to combat what was known as 'Chilitis' – diarrhoea and dysentery.

We dutifully took our pills, with the exception of centre-half Peter Swan, who couldn't be bothered. One night the locals arranged a concert – guitarists, dancers and singers – and Ray Wilson, one of the most popular players in the squad, persuaded us to attend. There was little else to do and we enjoyed it, particularly when Peter Swan was talked into going up on the stage to join in. A local photographer took pictures of him dancing with one of the girls.

Some pictures were wired back to England and used in the local Sheffield newspaper, and Peter's wife, who was in hospital having a baby at the time, was most upset when she saw it. A week later, Peter went down with stomach trouble and was taken to hospital. He was really very ill.

Ray Wilson and I went to visit him but were unable to find him in the ward. We eventually discovered him sitting in a toilet vomiting. When he saw us, he moaned: 'Here I am dying and my wife thinks I'm having a good time.' That morning a letter had arrived from his wife!

I had almost as much reason to be downhearted because I twisted an ankle while playing in a knockabout friendly game in Peru and was unfit for the whole tournament. In those days, England travelled without a team doctor. It was a mistake, as Peter Swan's illness showed.

There were some very good players in the England side, but once more we failed to pass the quarter-final stage. Johnny Haynes was still captain. Jimmy Armfield and Ray Wilson, two fine defenders, were the full-backs. Maurice Norman of Spurs, whose career was ended by a broken leg, and Ron Flowers of Wolves were the central defenders. In midfield with Haynes was Bobby Moore, while Bryan Douglas, a skilful, tricky winger, played on the right wing and Bobby Charlton on the left.

The front strikers were Gerry Hitchens, the former miner who was playing in Italy and qualified as the smartest dressed player in the party, and Jimmy Greaves, who was back in England with Spurs after his short and unhappy stay with AC Milan.

I shared a room with Jimmy Adamson, the Burnley player who was being groomed as an eventual successor to Winterbottom. When the chance came to take over, Jimmy turned it down and the FA turned instead to Alf Ramsey at Ipswich. England's opening game at Rancagua was disappointing, a 1–2 defeat against a Hungarian side which contained only goalkeeper Gyula Grosics from the great team of the fifties. A glorious individual goal by Florian Albert, successor to Hidegkuti, won the game for the Hungarians.

After beating Argentina 3–1, England could only draw 0–0 with Bulgaria and needed to beat Brazil to reach the semi-finals. Garrincha, the star of the 1962 World Cup, routed us in the quarter-final game at Vina del Mar, scoring twice and thumping a long-range free kick off Ron Springett's chest for Vava to score.

Ramsey's appointment from the professional ranks changed the set-up, and at last England became better organised under a full-time manager who was allowed to select the team he wanted.

Alf knew what he wanted and single-mindedly went ahead and did it. But after his success in winning the World Cup in 1966, he started running into the difficulties which have plagued English football ever since. The more successful clubs became more involved in European competitions and some were reluctant to lose their best players at crucial moments.

Until the First Division is reduced to eighteen clubs, I cannot see these problems being resolved. Only two or three clubs are affected each year, usually the same clubs like Liverpool, Ipswich, Arsenal, Leeds, Nottingham Forest and Manchester United, and the other clubs in the First Division naturally want to continue to play forty-two League matches each season and not lose income by reducing that total to thirty-six.

Six

Back at Craven Cottage

Craven Cottage was as I remembered it when I returned for training in the summer of 1962. The paintwork was the same colour. Tommy Trinder was still chairman. And the directors' box still had its quota of showbiz stars and personalities.

It was a social club but a very special club. It was a good place to work and I think I enjoyed my years there more than any other period in my playing career. No one felt threatened. There were no underground subterfuges going on. We lived with a sense of failure, because most seasons we were in the bottom half of the table fighting against relegation, but it didn't matter. It was a happy club. Maybe Fulham lacked the professionalism and ruthlessness of the big clubs who won trophies but there were many compensating factors.

Fulham were never going to win anything because although they had six or seven good players, Johnny Haynes, Alan Mullery, George Cohen, Graham Leggatt, Eddie Lowe and maybe myself, they also had some average players. They were always two or three players short of a good team, and had no money to go out and buy the players that were needed.

Johnny Haynes had just become the first £100-a-week player, but there was no jealousy. We knew he was worth the money. He was two players rolled into one. Perhaps he didn't get back and challenge for the ball, but if he had done that perhaps he would have been less effective when in possession.

One of the lesser players was Maurice Cook, the centre-forward bought from Watford. Maurice, or 'Cookie' as we knew him, was very popular with the rest of the players and also with the spectators. He was a whole-hearted player who occasionally scored some spectacular goals. Johnny Haynes made him the butt of his mickey-taking and 'Cookie' loved it. He carried Johnny's bag for him, and when we played golf, would carry his golf bag.

'Tosh' Chamberlain was still there, still telling stories, still smiling. There was a new manager, however, in Beddy Jezzard, a former player who grew up at the club. I liked him very much. It was impossible for anyone to dislike him. He was so nice you felt you had to work for him and give your best.

Sometimes when he had to show the iron fist, he became irate and that was his weakness. A manager must be firm but he cannot afford to upset himself too much. I think the game worried Beddy. He could be rather sensitive, and sometimes in football you cannot afford to be too sensitive.

In those days, Alan Mullery was a brash, Cockney lad who had a lot of confidence in his ability. He was an old fashioned wing-half – a player with a good dig in the tackle, a good passing sense and a competitive attitude. He was a very forthright person, a lad who never bothered to count to ten. I am not surprised he has become a successful manager. He had all the qualities. I wondered at one time whether his forthrightness might let him down, but it hasn't. It takes differing types of people to be managers. Brian Clough is the most forthright of all and it hasn't harmed his career. He has won plenty of trophies and built some fine sides.

My confidence in the Fulham board waned somewhat when they agreed to accept an offer for Mullery from Spurs manager Bill Nicholson in March 1964. Nicholson offered £72,500. He wanted a replacement for Danny Blanchflower and saw Mullers as the ideal man. Fulham accepted the bid because they said they needed the money. But it convinced the players that the club had no ambition. If they were going to sell the best players what chance did they have? We wondered who would be next. It was a time of disillusionment.

Mullery started so badly at White Hart Lane that I hoped Nicholson might be persuaded to change his mind and sell him back to Fulham. But Mullery persevered and finally established himself in the side. Fulham did eventually buy him back, but not until 1972.

We used to say about George Cohen: 'He's hit more photographers than Frank Sinatra.' George was quick and broke up the flanks exceptionally well, but his final ball was rarely on target. Usually he would hit his cross into the crowd, or into the photographers. George was a nice type of boy, a whole-hearted player with a good sense of humour and good social habits. Fulham always

produced players like that. We were delighted when he graduated to
the England team because he deserved it.

Graham Leggatt, the Scottish striker signed from Aberdeen, was
reluctant to pass – particularly in the box – but scored some unbelievable goals. He would be coming in on an angle, and with
everyone, including the goalkeeper, expecting a cross, would fire a
shot straight into the net with a brisk swing of the leg that had little
backlift. He was a little on the lazy side and I often complained to
him about his attitude. But he could speak his mind and was quite
intelligent. We didn't see much of him – once training was over, he
would be off home to his family. But because he scored so many
spectacular goals, he was very popular with the fans.

One of the funniest men on the staff was Dave Underwood, the
goalkeeper. Dave had this Bela Lugosi look and ready Cockney wit.
He was one of the bravest players I ever encountered. During a
game against West Bromwich Albion, Johnny Haynes put him in
trouble with a back pass, and as Dave went down for the ball John
Kaye, the Albion centre-forward, kicked him in the foot, breaking
his big toe.

Dave was the only fit goalkeeper at the club at the time and had to
continue playing. His toe was so swollen that he had difficulty
putting his boot on, yet he never complained. It was his right foot, so
when he had to kick the ball from his hands he used his left foot, and
the goal kicks were taken for him by one of the other players.

Jack McClelland, the Irishman from Arsenal, was another goalkeeper on the books around this time. He was a quiet lad, quite
unlike Dave Underwood or Tony Macedo, the first choice. Macedo
now lives in South Africa. He runs a goalkeepers' training school
and recently asked me if I was interested in taking any of his
youngsters. With the political situation as it is, I had to turn down his
offer.

Rodney Marsh started his career at Fulham, and I played with
him briefly before he was sold to Third Division Queen's Park
Rangers for £15,000. Even in those days, the mid-sixties, that was a
small amount of money for such a skilled player. But Vic Buckingham, who had succeeded Beddy Jezzard as manager, didn't
appreciate his talents. Vic thought he was too much of an enter-
tainer. One day we were training at the Bank of England sports
ground in Roehampton and Rodney was displaying his repertoire of
tricks. He could do some amazing things with the ball and was in full
flow when Vic suddenly stopped the training.

'Everybody in,' shouted Vic. We gathered round. Addressing Marsh, who was then still in his teens, he said: 'You are a ———— clown. Piss off.' Not long afterwards, Marsh was sold to Rangers.

I liked Rodney. He was a personable young lad and a good player. He may have become more of an individualist because of an accident at Leicester early in his career when he injured his ear in a collision with a defender while heading a goal. He fell over in the showers afterwards and it was obvious that his balance was affected. He was out of the game for some weeks, and when he returned, his hearing was never the same. He was awarded compensation by the Industrial Injuries Board.

At the time Marsh was sold, Buckingham went out and bought Allan Clarke from Walsall for £35,000. Clarke couldn't get into the side for a time because the front three of Steve Earle, Graham Leggatt and Les Barrett were playing so well. Steve Earle and Les Barrett were similar types, quick players who didn't relish being whacked by defenders. Barrett was a bit of a dreamer but, like Earle, did a good job for Fulham.

After being substitute for a number of matches, Clarke finally came on against Leeds in a Good Friday match in front of thirty-nine thousand fans at Craven Cottage. We were awarded a penalty, and, as the club penalty taker, I stepped up to put the ball on the spot.

As I walked back, Clarke came over and said: 'Very important, this one, son. Take your time.' He was nineteen and making his début, and I was thirty-two, an established international and one of the most experienced players in the country! But that was Clarkey – always cheeky and arrogant on the field. He was a loner and didn't get on with Vic Buckingham.

I admired him as a player. He was cool in the box, finished well and, for someone of his beanpole physique, was good in the air. He did his own thing then just as he does now as manager of Leeds. He learned a lot from Don Revie about containing football and freezing the game, and his negative tactics in his first season at Elland Road were justified, because he got the club out of trouble. Leeds were on the way out until he arrived.

Another player who was at Craven Cottage around this time who became a manager was Fred Callaghan, the left-back. I was surprised that 'Fiery' Fred went into management, first in non-League football and then with Brentford. I thought he would be too light hearted. He was always laughing and joking as a player. He used to

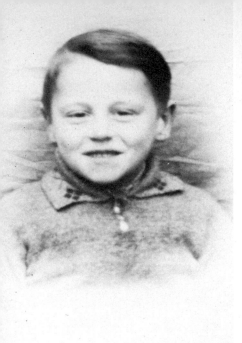

Above: The author aged four.

Above right: At the age of fifteen with brother Ron.

Right: A family group at Worcester Park in 1967. With my wife Elsie and the boys – Mark (on my knee), Andrew and Paul.

Tony Macedo saves from Geoff Hurst at Craven Cottage,
22 August 1964. Another World Cup player, George Cohen, has just
tackled him, and I am at the rear. Notice the fans sitting round the edge of
the pitch. Craven Cottage used to be full in those days!

Playing for an F A XI against a South African XI at Salisbury, Rhodesia –
before the days of blacklists and boycotts – I try to make a point to the
referee. Bill McGarry, Syd Owen and Peter Harris argued in vain, for my
shot had gone into the goal through a hole in the side netting.

This was how football clubs treated rib injuries twenty years ago. The size of the equipment may have changed, but the principle of using ultra-sonic treatment has altered little over the years. Fred Pedley was the WBA physiotherapist at the time.

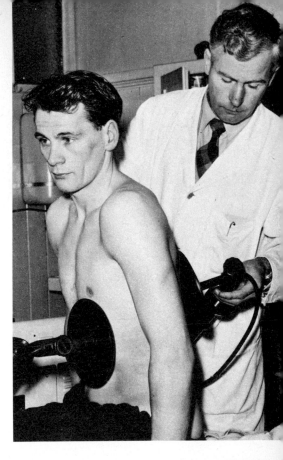

Below: Leaving Liverpool in 1959 for WBA's tour of Canada. On the right, with his hand on Maurice Setters' shoulder, is manager Vic Buckingham. That was about the only time Vic had Maurice under control! Back row (*left to right*): Chuck Drury, Joe Kennedy, Stuart Williams, Bobby Robson, Clive Jackman, Ray Barlow, Ray Potter, Dick Graham (trainer), Derek Hogg, Brian Whitehouse, Jim Gaunt (chairman), Vic Buckingham. Front row: Bobby Cram, Keith Smith, Alec Jackson, Archie Styles, Ronnie Allen, Dave Burnside, Graham Williams, Maurice Setters.

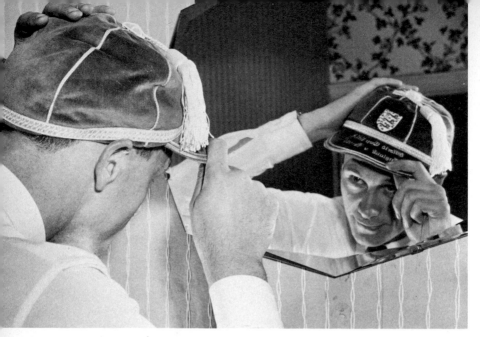

Trying on my first England cap – England v. France, 1957. I have twenty of those caps at home, but that was about the only time I have actually worn one!

My first goal for England, in the game against France at Wembley on 27 November 1957. With Robson netting a second, and Tommy Taylor also scoring twice, England won 4–0. The team was: Hopkinson, Howe, Byrne, Clayton, Wright, Edwards, Douglas, Robson, Taylor, Haynes and Finney.

Getting in a header in England's first match against the USSR in Russia. The date was 18 May 1958, and we drew 1–1. A month later we drew with them again, this time 2–2 in the World Cup in Sweden. It was the Russians who finally eliminated us from the tournament when we lost 1–0 nine days later in Gothenburg.

The England team which lost 3–0 to Spain in the Bernabeu Stadium, Madrid, on 15 May 1960. Back row (*left to right*): Jimmy Armfield, Bobby Charlton, Ron Springett, Bobby Robson, Peter Swan, Ron Flowers. Front row: Peter Brabrook, Johnny Haynes, Jimmy Greaves, Joe Baker, Ray Wilson.

Top: With Johnny Haynes and Brian Douglas at the first ever England training get-together at Lilleshall in 1961. Those candlewick track suits were very warm!

Above: A slight disagreement with Denis Law during a Manchester United v. Fulham match! Law was a very competitive player who could provoke this kind of response occasionally, but he was a great finisher and a wonderful player.

Below: Converting a penalty for Fulham against Ron Springett, the Sheffield Wednesday and England goalkeeper, at Craven Cottage.

The Fulham team that won the first ever *Daily Express* five-a-side championship. On my left are Jimmy Hill (before he grew his beard), Johnny Haynes, Ian Black and Eddie Lowe. Shorts were longer in those days!

With Allan Clarke, Fulham's outstanding player at the time – cheeky and arrogant on the field, but a loner off it. This was my first day as manager, and we were on the beach at Worthing trying an old-fashioned sea water cure on Allan's troublesome ankle.

Above: The Ipswich squad when I took over in 1969. Back row (*left to right*): Bobby Robson, Derek Jefferson, Charlie Woods, Ronnie Wigg, David Best, John O'Rourke, Bobby Bell, Mick McNeil, Cyril Lea. Middle row: Mick Mills, Mick Lambert, Colin Harper, Bill Baxter, Tommy Carroll, Ian Collard, Clive Woods. Front row: Steve Stacey, Peter Morris, Bobby Hunt, Frank Brogan.

Left: One of my most successful buys was Paul Mariner, seen here on the day I signed him from Plymouth Argyle in October 1976. Though most of my players came up through the ranks, I believe it is necessary for clubs to buy ready-made quality players occasionally.

be teased about his chin, which was as big as Jimmy Hill's, but he didn't grow a beard.

One of the whole-hearted enthusiasts on the staff was Bobby Drake, the son of former Arsenal and Southampton centre-forward Ted Drake. Ted was a blood and thunder centre-forward of the old style, a courageous player who was never deterred by the flying boots.

His son was almost as brave but never really made the grade. Very few sons of famous footballing fathers ever do, which is surprising when you consider all the advantages of being schooled by a father who knows the game. Perhaps the drive and ambition is missing. It is too easy. We give our sons footballs at an early age and spend a lot of time with them in the garden, but maybe that has a counter-productive effect.

None of our sons is a footballer, although they are all keen on the game. I regret that very much. Desiring to give them the best education we could, we sent them all to rugby-playing schools – Paul and Andrew to St George's College, Weybridge, and Mark to St Joseph's College, Ipswich. All three got into their first teams at rugby and cricket.

The change of manager did little to change Fulham's position at the wrong end of the First Division. After finishing fifteenth in 1963–4, we slumped to twentieth the following season and we were just one place off relegation again in 1965–6. The club was full of jokers and nice lads and it was a good place to work, but we were never going to trouble the teams at the top.

Mark 'Pancho' Pearson arrived from Manchester United to give us some aggression in midfield. Mark, with his long sideburns, had a reputation for being a dirty player, but I thought he was very fair. He tackled hard but never maliciously. In fact, I thought he was a delightful person, quite unlike his image. On the field, he was as hard as a diamond. Off it, he was as nice a fellow as you could meet.

The club was full of good types, lads like Stan Brown, a little whirlwind of a player who played in midfield then as sweeper, Jim Conway, the Irish winger, and John Ryan, a midfield player and full-back who was given a free transfer by Vic Buckingham. When I became manager of Ipswich I tried to sign Ryan, but Harry Haslam, then manager of Luton, beat me to it.

By 1967 I was beginning to think of what I would do for a living after my playing career was over. I was engrossed in coaching and wanted to stay in the game either as a coach or a manager. At thirty-four, I felt I was ready to make the change. I had a variety of offers. The first was from Arsenal. They wanted me as a player to add some experience to their side. The second came from Southend United, who wanted me as player-manager. Trevor Bailey, then a Southend director, interviewed me while Essex were batting in a match at Brentwood.

But the offer that appealed to me most came from an unexpected quarter – Vancouver in the far West of Canada. I had been there with WBA so I knew the area. It was one of the world's most admired cities, and, as I believed at the time, a convivial place to work.

The offer to become manager of a new club called Vancouver Royals was relayed by George Stirrup, the agent who acted on behalf of Real Madrid and several other leading continental clubs. The TV commentator Ken Wolstenholme was also involved in the talks I had with Stirrup over dinner at George's Wimbledon home. The salary was £7,000 a year, twice as much as I was making at Fulham. The Royals were to use the Empire Stadium in Vancouver, the arena made famous in 1954 by Jim Peters when he staggered towards the tape in the final of the marathon in the Empire Games.

I had an open mind. I felt it was a chance to be a pioneer in the development of soccer in America and thought it would be good experience for me. Elsie was a less keen. She would have preferred to remain at home. It meant taking our three boys out of school and emigrating to a new country.

After I decided to accept, we moved most of our furniture to a rented house in Vancouver and sailed via the Panama Canal, Los Angeles and Acapulco in the *SS Oriana*. We still retained our house in Worcester Park, Surrey. I had to build a new team from scratch for a consortium of business people headed by a Brigadier Aitkins, a retired soldier who won the DSO while serving in the Canadian Army.

Fulham sold me to the Royals for £10,000, a lot of money considering they paid £20,000 for me five years earlier and I was by now at the end of my playing career. On a limited budget, I had to find a team from somewhere.

I was allowed up to £6,000 a player and bought Bobby Cram from WBA, Peter Dinsdale from Huddersfield, John Green from Blackpool and Pat O'Connell and Henry Hill from Fulham. I also bought a goalkeeper from Cyprus recommended to me by Jack Kelsey, the ex-Arsenal goalkeeper, and two Chinese players I had seen in Hong

Kong. But four months before the season was supposed to open in March, I still hadn't got the team together. The Brig, as I called him, advised me to let the English players stay on in England for a while.

When my first two salary cheques hadn't arrived I guessed what was happening: the owners didn't have enough money to meet the bills. I was very disturbed. We had moved our house and family to the other side of the world, and now my job was in jeopardy. To solve the cash problem, the consortium called in George Flaherty, owner of the San Francisco Golden Gate Gales. Flaherty gave up his franchise in San Francisco and took over a fifty-one per cent share in the Royals. I learned that he had hired Ferenc Puskas, the former Hungarian and Real Madrid forward, as his coach at £10,000 a year – some £3,000 more than I was being paid. Puskas was gathering his own team together in Madrid where he had set up a training school. The Royals had no money ... but two football teams and two managers.

I was told to go to Madrid to join Puskas, and in November I went, leaving Elsie behind in a strange country with no friends. Puskas, whom I revered as a player, could speak no English and I found it was impossible to work with him. He may have been a great footballer but did not impress me as a coach. The training camp was a mess, just two old concrete huts in a field. Puskas had advertised for footballers and every day an odd collection of unknowns turned up in the hope of being signed.

Puskas's only idea of training seemed to be to get the 'players' to serve balls at him for him to volley at goal. There were Hungarians, Spaniards, a Dutchman and an amateur player from Liverpool. I wanted to take training sessions but Puskas insisted it was his right. However, it was impossible even to have an argument with him, because neither of us could speak the other's language.

I became increasingly depressed. By this time the English players I had signed were with me, and they were equally depressed. We were quartered in a third-rate hotel in Madrid, separated from our wives and families, and Christmas wasn't far away. I was in such a state of despair that I wrote to Allen Wade, the FA Director of Coaching, to seek his advice. He told me to stick it out until I returned to Vancouver and I had a chance to put the matter in the hands of my solicitor.

Eventually I managed to persuade Puskas to play a practice match, his players against mine, and my side won 9–2. It was pretty obvious that his players couldn't play. After I wrote to the Brig detailing my complaints, Flaherty flew to Madrid to try and sort everything out. I knew I would get no satisfaction from Flaherty. He knew little about football and worshipped Ferenc Puskas.

Some of Puskas's players complained to me that they had to pay ten per cent of their salary to Puskas as an agent's fee. Gerry Langindyke, a Dutchman who spoke good English, acted as interpreter. The players were on £6,000 a man, so if what they said was correct, £600 of that was going straight into Puskas's pocket.

When I told Flaherty about it he refused to believe me. He accused me of making it up to embarrass Puskas. 'Don't accept what I say,' I told him, 'speak to the players.' He refused. I spoke on the telephone to John Pickburn, the Royals' secretary in Vancouver, and told him I wanted to get home for Christmas. My English players also wanted to return home. Permission was finally granted, and when Elsie and the boys greeted me at Vancouver Airport I was never more relieved to see their faces.

Shortly afterwards, I saw Flaherty, who had also returned to Vancouver, and insisted that I be allowed to carry out the terms of my contract, which said I was the head coach. 'Make Puskas the Number 2', I said.

'I can't,' he said. 'I've promised him he can run the team.' He offered me all sorts of posts, from general manager to youth development officer for British Columbia. I rejected them all and said if I couldn't carry out the job I had been appointed to do I would sue. 'Okay, sue,' he said.

I saw a firm of lawyers and they told me I had a watertight case. The sum of £17,500 was at stake, and I was advised to sit at home and wait for the pay-out. I went out running at nights to keep fit. It was a miserable Christmas, the most depressing of my life, but my mood changed abruptly when I was rung by Graham Hortop, the Fulham secretary.

'We've heard about your problems,' he said. 'How would you like to return to Fulham?' I replied: 'I'm not fit. I haven't trained properly for months.'

'Not as a player. As manager,' he said. 'I'm offering you the job. Are you interested?' I was shocked . . . but very excited. When I told him I would accept, he said: 'Can you come tomorrow?' I said I could. Fulham's offer was £4,000 a year, just over half the money I was supposed to be getting with the Royals.

The lawyers told me that by taking a new job I would prejudice my chances of being paid out on my contract, but I didn't care. I left for London a few days later on my own. Fulham paid my fare and half my family's expenses. Vic Buckingham had just been sacked, and Fulham were bottom of the table. I couldn't wait to get started.

The Vancouver episode was the unhappiest period of my life. Of course the North American Soccer League has improved immeasurably since those days, but I still wouldn't work there. I cannot see football having a future in America until it is nationwide throughout the continent and is played at most schools. They have tried to graft the sport on to the existing sporting framework in America and it hasn't taken on yet.

We can learn from their promotional and marketing ideas but little else. They certainly sell the game there, whereas we expect people to simply turn up. But on the playing side they have nothing to show us. I don't think the shoot-out is a good idea. I think the draw should continue to have a place in our game. When, in the 1980–1 season, Ipswich went to Anfield and drew, we came home proud of our achievement, but we wouldn't have been in such a good mood had we lost a shoot-out.

Nor do I think the thirty-five-yard off-side line is a good idea. I have thought a lot about this. One of the ills of our game is the way both sides pack into a thirty-yard stretch of the field, denying each other space. There is no doubt that this diminishes the game as a spectacle and inhibits our players. But I feel there are still ways of overcoming the off-side trap – by intelligent running by forwards on to long passes from the rear, and by players using their dribbling ability to go it alone.

As it turned out, Vancouver Royals went bankrupt, so I wouldn't have been able to collect my money in any case. My lawyers told me I was tenth on the list of creditors and could not expect to receive much anyway. Puskas was a failure, as I thought he would be, and the team had only a moderate amount of success playing before dwindling audiences. My players fulfilled their contracts and two of them, Peter Dinsdale and Bobby Cram, are still living in Canada. Both are successful businessmen.

Fulham came out of the venture better than anyone. They had insisted on receiving the £10,000 transfer fee for me before I left, so they pocketed that and got a manager for nothing!

Seven

Number 686

I lasted just over nine months as Fulham's manager before I became the 686th manager to be sacked since the war. I will always remember that figure. In recent years there have been so many sackings that the total is rarely brought up to date, but in 1968 few firings took place without the public being told how many there had been since the Second World War.

Being dismissed as manager of a football club is a shattering experience. When the managing director of a company is sacked there is usually little publicity, but in football it is a vastly different matter. The newspapers are full of it. (In my case, they knew about it before I did.) You are public property. The whole nation knows about your predicament, and there is no dignity in it. You may have worked hard and diligently – I know I did – yet you are given your cards.

When it was confirmed that I had been dismissed, I walked out on to the Craven Cottage pitch, where I had played for twelve years and had such enjoyable times, and stood in the centre circle and cried. I am not ashamed to admit that. I looked round at the stands and vowed: 'I am never coming back to this place again.'

Of course I did go back, but my relationship with the people who made the decision to sack me was never the same. I had no more contact with them. Sir Eric Miller, the Jewish businessman who was the prime influence in my removal, later shot himself.

I was thirty-four when I started as Fulham manager on 23 January 1968. I was one of the younger managers, for in those days managers tended to be older than that. I knew little about Miller at the time of my appointment except that he was head of Peachey Property, a big development company, and appeared to be a very rich man.

None of the other directors were rich men and they recruited Miller because he could give the club financial backing. Miller would drive to the ground in a Lamborghini or a Ferrari. Sometimes he came in his own personal taxi. An incident later in that taxi really sealed my fate with Miller, as I shall explain.

Miller bought the taxi after standing in a London street one day and finding that it was hard to hail a taxi – he offered to buy the first one he managed to hire so the problem wouldn't arise again! He also reasoned that it was easier to park a taxi. He could always have the vehicle waiting for him.

Tommy Trinder offered me a three-year contract at £4,000 a year, which was £1,000 a year less than Johnny Haynes was receiving. I didn't mind. I was just glad to be back home and in a job. Graham Hortop, the secretary, drove me down to Worthing to meet the players where they were in training for the following Saturday's third round FA Cup tie against non-League Macclesfield. I knew all of them except Joe Gilroy, the Scottish full-back signed by Vic Buckingham.

Fulham were 1–2 down against Macclesfield and I could see that playing standards had fallen since I was last at the club. There was a tenseness in the crowd but no hostility. Crowds were much more placid in those days than they are now. Haynes rallied Fulham in the second half and my first game in charge ended in a 4–2 victory, but the signs were bad. The team lacked confidence and needed new players.

In particular we needed an experienced defender, and the directors approved the expenditure of £30,000 on Sheffield United's Reg Matthewson, a good, solid professional who never let us down. I spent most of my time driving to and from matches trying to find new players. I knew the club had little money to spend. The key to our First Division survival was Allan Clarke. The directors said if I could get him playing, we might avoid the drop.

Clarke didn't seem interested. I went to his house to attempt to talk him round. 'By staying here, I won't get an England cap,' he said.

'Oh really!' I said. 'I played for England. John Haynes played for England. George Cohen played for England. Alan Mullery played for England. If you're good enough, you'll get picked, whatever club you are playing for.'

He remained unconvinced. He scored twenty goals that season, the highest in the first team, but his contribution was below what I expected from him and his relations with the other players caused problems. There were enough problems with the club being bottom of the table without the star player being disaffected. . . .

Matt Busby, then manager of Manchester United, offered £150,000 in cash for Clarke, a British record transfer fee, but it was turned down because the directors agreed with me that once other clubs knew we had that kind of cash they would ask exorbitant amounts for any player we tried to buy as a replacement.

The news of Busby's offer soon leaked to the newspapers. Most big stories in football find their way into the daily papers. There seems to be no way of stopping that. Football League regulations forbid clubs from revealing fees but generally the amounts quoted are right. Sometimes managers will mislead reporters, giving them the impression that they have bought a bargain when they haven't. Generally, however, the facts are right. There are few secrets in professional football.

On transfer deadline day, 17 March 1968, I bought a player I thought we could use profitably after Clarke had gone – Johnny Byrne, the Crystal Palace striker. I had previously tried to buy John Toshack from Cardiff, but Toshack didn't want to leave home to live in London. He was earning twenty-five pounds a week at the time, a ridiculous wage for a player of his ability, but he was a shy, home-loving lad in those days and I failed to talk him round. The Fulham board had somehow agreed to raise £65,000 to buy him, much to my surprise.

Byrne, one of the finest touch players England has produced since the War, was twenty-eight at the time, cost £17,500 and was bought on a train! Crystal Palace were returning from Manchester, and Fulham were on the same train. Clubs still travelled by train at that time. Nowadays most of them use luxury coaches, often owning their own coaches as Ipswich do. It provides a better service and is quicker. More important, it enables the players to have privacy.

In today's conditions, it would be almost impossible for football teams to use the trains. The advent of the travelling football supporter has meant that trains are often packed with young football fans who are less well-mannered than the young men of my youth. Also, few trains serve meals on Saturdays.

Over a drink with Bert Head, the Palace manager, I agreed a deal for Byrne. The transfer forms had to be signed and a message telexed to the Football League headquarters in Lytham St Annes by midnight to enable Byrne to play in our remaining matches, and we beat the deadline by just ninety minutes.

Fulham managed to hold on to Clarke until the close season, not that it did the club much good. Tommy Trinder was always available for a quote and he said: 'Selling Clarkey is like asking a dying man to sell his watch. Everyone wants to plunder the corpse but I'm telling them we're not dead yet.'

The end was not long delayed. We mustered only twenty-seven points, five behind Sheffield United, and were relegated. The directors didn't seem to mind. We were bottom when I started and still bottom at the end of the season. They attached no blame to me, or so I thought.

Clarke attracted the attention of most of the big clubs. When a smaller, less successful club has a good young player – and Clarke was probably the best young striker in the country at the time – the pressure on it to sell is enormous. It has become far worse since freedom of contract was introduced. Most of the smaller clubs have to sell in order to survive. The transfer system has its faults but no one can deny it redistributes wealth within the Football League and enables all ninety-two runners to keep going in the annual race.

Liverpool offered Tony Hateley plus money; Leeds offered money; Nottingham Forest offered Joe Baker plus money; Manchester United were still in, but the offer we finally accepted on 11 June 1968, came from a surprising quarter, Leicester City.

What attracted me about the Leicester offer was that it included Frank Large, a centre-forward I thought could do well for us in the Second Division. The deal was £120,000 in cash plus Large, who was valued at £30,000. Frank was one of the bravest players I have ever seen and also one of the nicest people. He was outstanding in the air but his skill level was hardly in the Haynes class.

To pull the club out of its decline, I knew we had to re-organise from within so I sacked Arthur Stevens, the chief scout, and recruited Harry Haslam, manager of non-League Tonbridge, in his place. I had played with Arthur and it disturbed me a lot that I had to sack him. He was the first person I ever sacked. He had no contract but the club gave him some money.

He also had Tommy Trinder's expensive camel coat. Towards the end of Arthur's playing days, Trinder came into the dressing-room with it on and Arthur, a bluff, hard-swearing Cockney, said: '——— hell, what a coat you've got there.'

Trinder replied: 'Score a hat-trick today and it's yours.' Arthur was a regular goal-scorer but Trinder was confident his jocular bet wouldn't be lost. Early in the game, Arthur cut in on the right and shot past the opposing goalkeeper. He turned jubilantly to the directors' box and raised a finger. Later on, he scored another goal and raised two fingers. And to everyone's amazement, he went on to score a hat-trick. Trinder handed over the coat and it was the last time he made such grandiose promises!

Harry Haslam had recommended to us a young seventeen-year-old left-back named Malcolm Macdonald, and we bought him from Tonbridge for £1,000. Macdonald was born in Finlay Street, a few yards from Craven Cottage, and was a Fulham fan, but his mother went to live in Forest Row, Sussex, after the death of her husband and he started his footballing career with Tonbridge.

I saw at once that he had the potential to be an outstanding goal-scorer. He was very quick and had a thunderbolt of a shot in his left foot. In most of his early games he peppered the boards to the side of the goal but that didn't displease me. I knew it was only a matter of time before he started getting them on target. He was a brash, cocky lad. He came in against Crystal Palace and ended our run of 630 minutes without scoring a goal. He could have had six. It was around this time that Sir Eric Miller began interfering. One day he said to me: 'Do you want Cliff Jones?' I said: 'I haven't given it any thought but my first reaction is possibly yes, perhaps he might do us some good.'

'Good,' he replied. 'I think we should try him.' Miller may have known the property market but he didn't know the value of footballers, and although I was slightly suspicious of his attitude, I did not suspect that he was now trying to run a football club as well as a business empire.

I was invited round to Miller's sumptuous house in The Boltons, Kensington, to have a chat about the deal and other possible deals. I thought it was irregular that a director should be taking the initiative in matters that should really have concerned the chairman, but Hortop assured me: 'Mr Trinder says it's all right.'

Cliff Jones had invested his money in two butchers' shops but the businesses had failed, leaving him with large debts. To restore his position, Tottenham Hotspur had agreed to let him have a free transfer and that any money they might receive would go direct to Jones. It was the start of legalised signing-on fees, with the money being spread over the period of the player's contract.

Previously players often asked for 'readies', or cash in the hand, which was illegal, and some clubs used to pay it. This made it extremely difficult for honest clubs who kept to the rule book when buying players. Most managers welcomed the change, providing it didn't mean that players asked for too much money as signing-on fees.

Cliff Jones was a deserving case. He was nearly thirty-three and, though nearing the end of his career, was still a good player. He was a superb lad, ideal for a dressing-room that was low in morale after an indifferent start to the season. Nearly a dozen clubs wanted him and I was delighted when he chose Fulham.

Frank Large didn't make the impact I expected and I signed Vic Halom from Orient for £30,000 as his replacement. Ten minutes after Halom signed, Brian Clough, then manager of Derby, arrived. Halom's career might have worked out differently if he had delayed signing!

My first dispute with Miller arose over my decision to drop Johnny Haynes. I felt Haynes was well past his best, and in our position we needed players who played when the other side had the ball. Miller was appalled when I told him.

'You can't do that,' he said. 'It's madness.' I said: 'We have to play without him. He's not going to last forever. The time has come to change the faces, and play new men. I am going to do it eventually, so why not now?' I said we needed a different approach in midfield. He thought the crowd would be upset, but as it transpired, they weren't.

Shortly afterwards he came back and said: 'I've found the mid-field player you want.' I said: 'Oh yes, who?' 'Eddie Bovington of West Ham. He will give us what we need and I can arrange it for you.'

'With all due respect, he's not what we want,' I said. I didn't know at the time that Miller was not only a friend of the Prime Minister, Sir Harold Wilson, but a friend of Bobby Moore, the West Ham captain.

'We don't want Bovington,' I said. 'He's a hard, physical crunch player and not the type we need. We don't want West Ham reserves. He will be no good to us.'

Miller's face hardened. Looking back after my dismissal, I realised that that was the moment when I lost my job. A few days later Miller came back to me.

'Will you do something for me?' he asked. 'Watch Eddie

Bovington play.' I was as polite as I could be. 'I've seen him play,' I said. 'I've played against him. I know what he is like.'

Later that same week I saw Miller again and he said: 'Listen, come and see Bovington with me. If you don't like him, that will be the end of it.' To curtail the saga, I agreed reluctantly and we went together in his taxi to Upton Park with Harry Haslam to see West Ham reserves take on Chelsea reserves in a London Challenge match.

Bovington was marking Barry Lloyd, and Lloyd scored a hat-trick in a 3–3 draw, which was an indication of what kind of game Bovington played that night. As we came down the corridor from the guests' lounge afterwards, we bumped into Moore. 'Hello Eric,' he called out to Miller, and the two of them spent some time talking together. I sensed what had happened. Bobby Moore was recommending Miller to buy his friend Bovington.

As we got into the taxi in the car park, Miller said to Harry Haslam and me: 'Isn't Bovington a good player? I thought he played well.' 'What?' I said. 'I thought he was poor on the night. We don't want him.'

Miller said irritably to his driver: 'Let's go.' The taxi was just emerging into the roadway when we saw Dave Sexton, the Chelsea manager, rushing out to catch the underground to Victoria before taking a train to his home in Brighton. Miller saw him and told the driver to stop.

'Hello, David,' he said. 'Can we give you a lift? We can drop you off at Victoria.'

Sexton got in. Miller knew him because Lady Miller was a season ticket holder at Chelsea and he sometimes attended matches at Stamford Bridge himself. We started talking about the game and Sexton said: 'What about that fellow Bovington? Lloyd ran rings round him.'

Miller stiffened, and the conversation dried up. After Sexton got off at Victoria, Miller rounded on me. 'I know you,' he said angrily. 'You primed him to say that.' I said: 'Good grief. Do you think I arranged for Dave Sexton to run out of the car park at that precise moment? You stopped to pick him up, not me.'

Shortly afterwards Fulham played at Carlisle and lost 2–0. Miller flew to the game in his private executive jet and took Johnny Haynes back with him. I didn't think there was any significance in that, as Haynes said his father was ill and he needed to return home as quickly as possible.

The following Thursday I was in my office at lunchtime when I got a call from Bernard Joy, the soccer writer of the *Evening Standard*. 'Are you all right?' he asked. I wondered what he meant. 'I mean about your job,' he said.

'What have you heard?' he asked. 'There's a rumour going around that you are going to lose your job.' 'I don't know anything about it,' I answered. 'No one's told me.'

David Miller of *The Daily Telegraph*, whom I had coached at Oxford University, rang a little later and he had obviously heard the same rumour. I gave him the answer I gave Joy.

Next door Hortop was working in his office and I went in and asked if he had heard anything. 'No,' he said. 'I've heard nothing. But you always get these stories when a club isn't doing so well.'

I left the club at five and before driving home to Weybridge, stopped on Putney Bridge to buy a *Standard*. There were big head-lines on the back page. 'FULHAM TO SACK ROBSON?' it said.

I was in a nervous state about it when I arrived home. 'If there's nothing in it, why hasn't one of the directors rung me?' I said to Elsie. By nine o'clock I could stand it no longer. Trinder was in Australia and I didn't know Miller's home number, so I rang Chappie D'Amato, one of the oldest directors.

'I'm ringing to get some peace of mind,' I said. 'There are stories in the papers that I'm to be sacked. Can you tell me anything?' There was a long silence. I knew the reports were true.

Finally, D'Amato said: 'Bobby, the news isn't very good.' 'That's a nice way to get to know – in the papers,' I said bitterly. He asked me to come into the ground at 10.30 in the morning to meet the directors.

Next day, Miller, D'Amato, Tony Dean and Hortop were in the office as I arrived. Miller confirmed the sacking. He offered me £4,000 as a settlement on the remainder of my contract which had more than two years to run. I didn't know what to do. I declined the offer. Later they agreed to increase the amount to £5,000, and I accepted. I told them I had turned down several offers to write my story in the Sunday newspapers. The offers were considerable, but I told them that wasn't the way I conducted negotiations. I never used it as a threat.

Harry Haslam and Roy McCrohan, my coach, were also sacked. They were less fortunate. Not being on contracts, they were paid just two weeks' wages. Later in my managerial career I always made a point of putting my staff on contract so that if they were sacked, they were amply compensated.

When I returned home, Bill Dodgin, who lived nearby, was there with Elsie. 'What's happened?' said Elsie. 'I've been sacked, love,' I said. Bill looked twitchy. He was working at QPR and had tried to buy Haynes from us.

He told me he had been employed by Fulham from that day as a coach, which was news to me. 'If you're the coach, who's the manager?' I said. 'John Haynes,' he said. I then realised why Haynes had flown back with Miller from Carlisle. It had been a put-up job carried out behind my back.

'Haynesey can't do the coaching, so he's taken me on,' said Dodgin. I felt no resentment against Johnny Haynes. Miller had used him – and it proved a mistake, because Haynes lasted just one month. He wasn't managerial material. He didn't like the office work and he didn't like coaching. Within a few months he quit Fulham after twenty years and went to play for Durban City in South Africa.

At the end of the 1968–9 season Fulham went down again, this time to the Third Division, and they remained there for two seasons until they were promoted in 1970–1. By that time Miller had more important matters to occupy him.

From Australia, where he was working in cabaret, Tommy Trinder said: 'You can't sack eleven players, but you can sack the manager, which is what we did. I'm sorry about it. We couldn't afford Bobby the time to prove himself. Perhaps he may prove us wrong at another club.'

I can understand why football clubs who need money look to someone like Eric Miller to help them, but it is a dangerous way of conducting their affairs. I don't believe rich men who have no footballing background should be allowed to buy their way into football clubs and control them. Certainly not property developers who may have ulterior motives.

Football clubs should be run by businessmen who employ professionals to look after the day-to-day affairs and the team. The set-up at Ipswich is the ideal one. The directors are all experienced businessmen who make the appointments and then let the professionals get on with it.

Eight

Ipswich

For nearly three months in the winter of 1968–69 I was unemployed. The previous twenty years I had worked every day, and it
was a new experience for me to wake and think: 'What am I going to
do today?' In those twenty years I hardly had a day off through
illness. Fortunately I am like my father: I never seem to fall ill.

I was in an anomalous position because we had just moved into a
house at Ripley in Surrey to be near the boys' school, St George's
College. It was stockbroker-belt country. The Beatles lived not
far away at Weybridge, and Mark, who was seven, used to ride
his bike past Ringo's house and rush back to say: 'I've just seen the
Beatles.' I walked our retriever Pip on St George's Golf Course for
two hours or more a day. We were living in a rich man's area,
yet I was unemployed and without any income coming in each
week.

I was too proud to go to the local office of the Social Security
Department to claim my dole money. I thought only layabouts and
social misfits claimed dole money. But as the weeks went on and my
savings dwindled I said to myself: 'This is crazy.' I went to the office
to sort out my position. While I was away in Canada, I forfeited any
claim to national insurance, so there was a certain amount of red
tape to disentangle before I could draw my first pay cheque from the
State – a money order for twelve pounds.

It is a humbling experience, joining the dole queue. Luckily no
one recognised me, and I was shaken when I saw the people who
were with me – bank managers, professional people and an Army
major. There was no disgrace, I soon learned, in being unemployed.

The telephone rang only occasionally, and I became more and
more despondent. My managerial career had only just started and it
seemed to have ended prematurely. I reflected on the offer West
Bromwich Albion made me during my final days as a player at

Fulham. Jim Gaunt, the Albion chairman, rang one day and offered me the manager's job. Jimmy Hagan had just been sacked.

I drove up to Gaunt's house and the whole Albion board were there. Gaunt said: 'The job is yours, but there will be no contract.' 'What!' I said. 'No contract?'

'No contract, that's right,' said Gaunt. 'We've just been caught and we're not being caught again. We gave Jimmy Hagan a five-year contract and he's left after only a year. We've had to pay out a lot of money.'

'You can't blame me for that,' I said. 'That's your problem. You want me on a week-to-week basis. Suppose I start badly? Within three months you could turf me out. I want some security. You know me. Give me a two-year contract and I won't let you down.'

Gaunt, a bluff Black Country businessman, was adamant. 'We want you to come back and have fire in your belly,' he said. 'But no contract!' I volunteered to accept a lower salary if I could have a contract, but he turned down my suggestion. Vancouver had offered me more money, but I would have preferred a job in England. Albion wanted someone on a trial basis. If I failed, there would be many more people behind me, just as desperate to break into soccer management. It was a slave trade way of running a business and I was very angry about it.

I was more upset when I learned that Alan Ashman, who was given the job, was put under contract. Ashman didn't have my playing experience and came from a small club, Carlisle. But he lasted a long time – five years.

The only offer I received when I was unemployed came from the Norwegian club Rosenberg, but I didn't want to go to Norway. I had three young children and they were all settled in schools in England. If I was to make a success of management, it had to be in the Football League.

Christmas was rapidly approaching and I was determined that the family would have an enjoyable festive season. We were without a television set at the time and although I had little money, I rang a rental company and ordered a seventeen-inch set. It was delivered on 23 December. First, I had to fill in a form, and in answer to the question 'What is your employment?' I wrote 'unemployed'. The lad who brought the set looked sceptically at me as he asked for the four months' rent in advance. I gave him the eighty pounds and we had a good Christmas. It was the first Christmas I had had at home for twenty years.

One interminably long day, Dave Sexton, then manager of Chelsea, rang and asked whether I would like to do some part-time scouting for him. When you are off the roundabout this is the time when you need your friends, and I shall always be grateful to Dave for thinking of me at the lowest point in my career.

Bertie Mee, who was in charge at Arsenal, also rang with a similar offer, but I felt it was unfair to work for two clubs so I turned down his kind approach. My first assignment for Dave was to watch the Ipswich v. Nottingham Forest match for him. I hadn't been to Portman Road since I last played there some years before. When I arrived, it suddenly occurred to me that both clubs were without a manager, and as an out-of-work manager myself, people connected with both clubs would think I was touting myself around. The thought of doing that embarrassed me and I tried to keep out of the way.

When I made a brief appearance in the boardroom at the end before dashing off to catch the first available train back to London, one of the Ipswich directors, Murray Sangster, came over and said: 'Hello, you are Bobby Robson, aren't you? How are you?'

Bill McGarry had resigned and Cyril Lea, the trainer, was in charge of the side. Forest had sacked Johnny Carey and Bill Anderson was temporarily in charge. Ipswich lost 2–3 but looked a reasonable side. Two midfield players, Colin Viljoen and Danny Hegan, impressed me and Ray Crawford was still a useful striker.

On the train home I thought it might be worthwhile applying for the manager's job at Ipswich as it had been advertised in the Press. I had no illusions of grandeur. In my position, Manchester United or Leeds were unlikely to come calling at my door. I had to take what I could get and Ipswich, though a small, homely club with limited money, were after all a First Division club.

Next morning I wrote a letter of application and posted it. Forty-eight hours later the phone rang and a voice said: 'This is John Cobbold of Ipswich.' Mr John, as everyone calls him at Ipswich, seemed slightly nervous and he stammered a little. 'I just thought I would like to tell you that we have received your letter,' he said. 'It is receiving consideration and we will contact you again.'

I thought it was decent of him to ring. Two days later he rang again and asked if I would like to attend an interview. We arranged a rendezvous at the Great Eastern Hotel the following Sunday lunch-time. There had been speculation in the newspapers about who were the candidates for the job and the names of Frank O'Farrell and Billy Bingham were foremost in the opinion of most columnists.

O'Farrell, then at Torquay, was quoted as saying that if he was to leave it would be for a club with potential, and he obviously didn't think Ipswich had that potential. As for Bingham, he said he preferred to remain at Plymouth.

When I met Mr John I asked about a contract and he replied: 'No, not really. We prefer not to give contracts.' He must have seen the disappointment in my face because he added: 'But you can take it from me that you will have two years at the club.'

I felt he was a man who could be trusted and I accepted their offer. After all, I was in a weak bargaining position. FLESA, the managers' association, is trying to make contracts a compulsory condition of employment and their executives are also trying to put pressure on clubs to pay out contracts in full when managers are sacked. But there is little chance of managers receiving the money that is due to them because, unlike most professions, football managers as a body lack solidarity.

If every manager or would-be manager said he wouldn't apply for a job until the last manager had been paid up satisfactorily, this irksome business of managers having to wait for their money, or accept a reduced sum, would be cleared up overnight. But too many candidates are waiting to step in. There is too much selfishness among managers. They abandon principles for the sake of a job.

With one exception, the directors who appointed me that day are still on the Ipswich board, which must be some kind of record in the Football League. The exception was Chris Robinson, who died. The only other change is that Patrick Cobbold is now chairman instead of John, but John is the vice-chairman, the two men having merely swapped positions. There have been no attempted coups, no power struggles. That is how a board of directors should operate. There should be continuity and stability, but this is rarely achieved in professional football.

I didn't make an auspicious start on my first day at Ipswich which incidentally was 13 January 1969. My train was due at Ipswich station at 9.45 but arrived thirty-five minutes late, and I was too late to supervise the training. Cyril Lea did that and I met the players afterwards. I realised very quickly that I would need to strengthen the squad. There were too many players over the age of thirty like Bill Baxter, the captain, Tommy Carroll and Ray Crawford, and some of the others weren't up to First Division standards.

Bill McGarry had done a good job keeping them in the First Division and had left a strong sense of discipline. I didn't have to come in and lay down a lot of rules and regulations. The disciplinary code was all there – perhaps too much of it.

When a new manager arrives, he often has to clamp down and impose his personality on the club, but I had no call to do that. Bill McGarry was a tough disciplinarian who created a harsh brand of law and order inside the club. The players were frightened of him and some trembled in his presence. If a player made a mistake, or did something he didn't like, Bill would go up to him in a threatening manner, hold his fist under his chin and say: 'Don't do that again!'

Time was time and no one was ever late. No one abused him back and when he left, probably because he felt he could go no further with limited resources and no cash, it was like the lid being removed from a Jack-in-the-Box. Up jumped Jack and he wanted his say. McGarry had not long previously signed a long-term contract and it must have been a surprise to some supporters when he left to take over at Wolves, a club which had pioneered sound disciplinary habits under Stan Cullis. He was less successful at Molineux because he had better players to deal with, and some of them, like Derek Dougan, answered back.

I had no trouble in those early days with training sessions. The players appeared to like my ideas and no one objected to the fact that I was still young enough to look on some of them as contemporaries. We went to Everton for my first match in control and drew 2–2, Crawford punching in the equaliser with his fist and the referee failing to spot it.

Then, at Portman Road, we beat a Manchester United side containing Law, Charlton and Crerand 1–0, and also won at Arsenal. With the players available to us, these were miraculous results, but I reasoned that a team always does well when a new manager arrives because the players are out to show him what they can do. It's the second year that is the vital one. We ended the season in eighteenth position, a creditable end to a season of struggle.

Most of the early difficulties I had came from Baxter, a moody, dour Scot whom Cyril Lea warned me about, and the wives. Cyril said: 'He's a difficult customer but the best defender the club's ever had.' One day in training Baxter refused to carry out an order and I sent him off the field. It wasn't the first time I'd had trouble from him. I told him I was leaving him out of the next match, at West

Ham, and he was very angry. He asked: 'Why don't you fine me?'

'That wouldn't hurt you,' I replied. 'The way to hurt you is to prevent you from playing.'

Crawford, a nice, easy-going fellow, came to see me and said McGarry had promised him a free transfer at the end of the season. 'I can't give you away,' I said. 'You're still a good player!'

I could handle Crawford ... but his wife Eileen proved more difficult. She rang me one day and said: 'Hey, what are you doing ––––––– my husband around?' It was a new experience for me, being abused in Smithfield Market language by a woman! Crawford left at the end of that season. I sold him to Charlton for £12,500, which was good money in those days (ground admission was only 25p, and the most expensive seats 45p). Later when he played for Colchester, Dick Graham used to regale me with tales of his running battle with Mrs Crawford. But I must say in her defence that when I invited former players and their wives to my testimonial match in 1980 she was marvellous. Experiencing life at the other end of the football scale had softened her.

Another wife who gave me a hard time was the wife of Steve Stacey, a coloured defender from Wrexham. Steve was such a poor player that he was loaned to three Third and Fourth Division clubs and none wanted him, and when he played at Liverpool a wag shouted: 'Where did you get him from?' I left him out of the side, as any manager would, and his wife gave an interview to the local newspaper in which she claimed that I was racially prejudiced!

But the most irritating events concerning wives happened at the end of season in Cyprus, when I took a party of fifty-seven players, wives and officials on a club holiday. It was not my idea, but McGarry had apparently promised the players a holiday and they held the board to it. We played three matches to cover the costs, but the visit was a disaster from the start when the wives started arguing among themselves and with me.

Some of the complaints were so petty that it was unbelievable. One wife moaned that someone else had been seated nearer the balcony than she and her husband and it wasn't fair. Another said the beds in their room were less comfortable than their neighbours'. It was impossible to please them, and I vowed never to take wives abroad again.

It seemed that whatever I did I would never win some of the older players over. As soon as I disposed of one player's problems, another player would be waiting for me. One objected to the treatment he had been prescribed by the club doctor and threatened to sue the doctor. When I told the doctor, he said: 'That's all right, I'll sue him back!'

Every time there was an incident, it finished up in headlines in the national newspapers. We had a mole, or several moles, inside the camp. It was as though a group of players were determined to get rid of me. It was them or me, and I decided very early on that it wasn't going to be me.

One player I had difficulty with was John O'Rourke, the centre-forward. O'Rourke was a flash type, a Jack the lad, but a very useful goal-scorer and a good player. He was one of the laziest players I have encountered in the game, so lazy in fact that he made Jimmy Greaves look like the biggest workhorse in football.

O'Rourke was caught off-side more times than any forward I have known. That was because he was always hanging upfield waiting for the ball and wasn't sharp enough to spot defenders moving up to catch him out. But for all that he could score goals. He had his good points.

He was a player who talked a lot to opponents during a match. He would ask them what they were earning, or what bonus they were on. At half-time, he would say: 'Hey, you do know what this lot are on?' I would reply: 'What's that got to do with us? You get on with your game.'

One day in training I was dissatisfied with his attitude and sent him to the dressing-rooms. 'I want my cards!' he said. 'All right,' I said. 'You can have your cards. Come to the office tomorrow morning and they will be there waiting for you.'

After training I told Walter Gray, the club secretary, what had happened and asked him to have O'Rourke's cards ready for collection. Ipswich would still retain his registration in any case, and he wouldn't have been able to play for another club. Next morning there was no sign of O'Rourke. The following day he showed up for training in the usual way. He was trying to test me.

On another occasion we were playing a match at the Hawthorns against my old club West Bromwich Albion and O'Rourke failed to arrive for a team meeting at five p.m. on the evening of the game. At 5.30, he strolled into the room. 'Where have you been?' I demanded. 'I've been for a walk,' he said. I was so angry that I withdrew him from the side although we only had twelve players with us and it meant that the coach, Cyril Lea, who still retained a players' registration, would have to be the substitute. Cyril hadn't played for two years, and as luck would have it, Bill Baxter was injured and had to come off, so Cyril had to go on.

From being 2–0 up, we held on to draw 2–2 but I was determined to make the same decision again if a similar situation arose. The players weren't going to flout my instructions like that. Shortly afterwards, I sold O'Rourke to Coventry for £80,000, which was a sound piece of business in the circumstances. In those days I had to wheel and deal for players, and most times it worked and Ipswich finished up in profit.

It was easy to say that I should have sold all the dissident players, but we couldn't afford to let anyone go without replacing him at a lesser cost. Ipswich were £40,000 in debt when I arrived, and that was a vast sum of money for a small club in those days. I had to do the weeding-out process gradually.

Bill McGarry left behind some solid characters, which I was grateful for, and one of the most reliable was the defender Derek Jefferson, a Geordie from Morpeth. Derek liked a drink and some-times could become boisterous, but he never let me down on the field. He was a whole-hearted player and a great tackler in the Nobby Stiles mould. He also shared a common deficiency with Nobby: he was very short-sighted and had to wear glasses. I think that explained the waywardness of some of his tackles. He didn't kick opponents deliberately.

Bill McGarry wanted to buy him from me, and when I knew that I had Kevin Beattie ready to come in as a replacement, I let him go for £80,000. There were some players I knew I had to ditch, but most of the staff were good types – players like Micky Mills, David Best, Geoff Hammond, Colin Harper, Peter Morris, Frank Clarke, Ian Collard, Bryan Hamilton, Colin Viljoen, Clive Woods and Trevor Whymark.

Tommy Carroll, the Dublin-born right-back, was next to antagon-ise me. He walked out and returned to Dublin over a minor issue and I was forced to suspend him. He was a good player, a great tackler, very fair with it and an excellent server of the ball. But he and his friend Bill Baxter didn't like me, and it showed. On his return to the club, I left him and Baxter out for a home game against Leeds which we lost 2–4.

The pair of them were laughing in the dressing-room afterwards, and what really upset me was when they sent a message in from the players' room later saying they wanted a bottle of champagne to celebrate our defeat. The following Friday, I again left the pair of them out. Carroll went up to the team sheet on the wall, saw that he wasn't in, and ripped it down and thrust it into my face.

'Here,' he said, 'stuff your ——————— team!' As he had made the first aggressive move I felt entitled to hit back, and soon we were exchanging blows. I couldn't back down. The rest of the players were watching and gauging my reaction. Baxter joined in and Cyril Lea came to my aid.

Geoff Hammond, the big right-back, stepped in between us and broke up the fight. As Carroll and Baxter made off, I stormed at Hammond: 'You big clown! Never do that again! I was beginning to enjoy myself. He hit me first. I was within my rights to have a go back and show him who is boss!'

Neither Carroll nor Baxter played in the first team for me again. Baxter was sold to Hull City for £12,500, and Carroll to Birmingham for £20,000. The other players were so disturbed by what had gone on that some of them asked if Baxter and Carroll could be made to change in the groundsman's hut, away from the rest of the team. I told them I couldn't do that. Baxter and Carroll could have complained to the PFA, quite justifiably, that they were being victimised. Until I sold them, I had to treat them the same as any other player.

What did please me in the aftermath of the Baxter–Carroll affair was the short statement issued to the Press by the players themselves saying they backed me and wanted an end to the unrest at the club. The departure of Baxter and Carroll was a turning-point in my career. The team was changing slowly, with more of my players taking over from the ones left behind by McGarry. One of the departures was Danny Hegan, the Scottish inside-forward whom I sold to WBA for £90,000, which included £25,000 in part exchange for Ian Collard. Hegan was a very gifted player, but he drank too much. He was no trouble to me except that he was always asking for a move.

If Hegan was with me now, I feel confident I could hold on to him because I am established and Ipswich are one of the best clubs in the country. But in those days he was hankering to play for a big club and Ipswich wasn't big enough for him.

Another significant date in my life was the day we played Manchester United in a night match and loss 1–3 at home. The date was 7 September 1971 and it was the second round of the League Cup. George Best played as a centre-forward and tore us apart, scoring two of the goals. He was unstoppable, brilliant. We had him marked man to man with cover behind, but it still didn't work. His genius was never more eloquently expressed than it was that night.

The capacity crowd failed to see the obvious: that we were the victims of a great player who was playing at his peak. They thought I was responsible. 'Robson out, Robson out!' they chanted, and that only made our players feel worse. Elsie was sitting in the stand and she couldn't believe it.

I feared the inevitable when a board meeting was called the next day. But John Cobbold started the meeting by saying: 'Gentlemen, the first business of the day is to officially record in the minutes the apologies of this board to our manager for the behaviour of the fans last night. Agreed? Right, on to the next business.'

I was very pleasantly surprised, and more so when the directors authorised me to spend £90,000 on Allan Hunter from Blackburn Rovers. Hunter, who actually cost £60,000 plus Bobby Bell, rated at £30,000, was one of my best signings. He was like a rock, and when he and Kevin Beattie were together I used to think we would never be beaten. In the seventies they were by far the outstanding players in their positions in the country.

It was distressing to me when Beattie had to retire because of his knee injury. I ranked him as the finest player ever produced by Ipswich, one of the best British players in post-war football. At his peak, when he was fit, he was awesome. He had so much pace and power, and in the air there was no one in the world to match him. Nat Lofthouse wasn't as good in the air, nor, probably, was Tommy Lawton. I didn't see Dixie Dean, so I cannot judge him. But for me, Beattie was the king when the ball was in the air. His left foot was a hammer. He had everything, and it was a tragedy for England when he began to have trouble with his knee right at the start of his international career. If Beattie had stayed fit, England's World Cup record in recent years might well have been much better.

Beattie had a testimonial in the 1981–2 season, and it was typical of him that he let Allan Hunter have his testimonial game first. Hunter realised £25,000 from his game against Celtic and he deserved every penny of it.

Beattie gave me some anxious moments off the field in his time at Portman Road – not because he was a bad lad, but because he tended to be gullible in his younger days. There was the incident in 1974 when he failed to turn up for an Under-21 game in Aberdeen at the appointed time. The first I knew about it was when Don Revie rang me and said: 'Where's Kevin Beattie?'

I replied: 'I don't know. I took him to the station personally this morning and he should be there by now. I've never taken a player to the station in my car before, but I did this time. The trains must be held up. Be patient. He'll show.'

Several hours later Revie rang again. 'He's not turned up,' he said. I had a feeling he might have gone home to Carlisle, as he had shown signs of being homesick in the past. I rang John Carruthers in Carlisle and asked him to drive to the Beattie's house, as they weren't on the telephone. Sure enough, Kevin was there. When the train arrived at Crewe, he got off and caught a connection to Carlisle. I told John to get him to a call-box and make a reverse charge call to me. By this time the news of his disappearance had reached the newspapers and everyone wanted to know what had happened to him.

When he eventually called I said: 'What's happened, son? What are you doing? You're prejudicing your international future.' He couldn't offer a sensible explanation except to say that he felt under pressure and needed to go home to see his parents. Next day the papers had a photograph of him sitting in a pub drinking a pint and playing dominoes with his father.

I spoke to him again on the telephone. 'You know what my father would have done,' I said. 'He would have given me a right spanking and put me on the first train to join the England team.' I felt his family hadn't helped him. John Carruthers, however, did an excellent job and persuaded Beattie to return.

By then the damage had been done. He was known as the footballer who ran away, and in our next few matches he was ribbed unmercifully by the supporters of the opposing team. I remember one game at Stoke when the fans were particularly cruel. They chanted 'Beattie wants his mummy' every time Kevin touched the ball. It was upsetting to him, but part of his maturing process.

Beattie's accident with a bonfire at his home on Easter Sunday, 1977, probably cost us the championship that season. We were two points ahead of Liverpool with a game in hand, but without Beattie's services we finished third, five points behind Bob Paisley's team. Beattie threw some petrol on to the fire to liven it up, and flames shot back into his chest and throat. He didn't play again that season.

Some players go through their careers without serious injury and manage to avoid trouble. But Beattie tended to walk straight into it. He was a buccaneering type of player who met every challenge head-on.

In my first four years at Portman Road I sold twenty-eight players, replacing them with modest buys and youngsters like Beattie, George Burley, Brian Talbot, Roger Osborne and Eric Gates, who came up through the youth scheme. Gates was another player who 'disappeared'. He played in our FA Youth Cup side in 1973 and I always believed he would make the grade. The snag was that we couldn't be sure where he would settle in the side – as an attacking midfield player or as a striker. He played in spurts and I felt he wasn't helping himself, which was why he was used as a substitute more than most players.

I thought he was on the verge of breaking through to the first team when in November 1978, Neal Manning, the football reporter of the local newspaper, rang to tell me that Gates had walked out of the club, adding: 'He says he's not coming back until he plays in the first team.'

I replied: 'He's not going to pressure me. I can't guarantee anyone a first-team place – Hunter, Beattie, Mariner, any of them.' Gates was staying with his family in Durham and was making money potato-picking. I called him and he repeated that he wasn't coming back unless I put him in the first team. I told him the only way he could prove he was worth a place was to return to the club. Meanwhile, I suspended and fined him.

I felt his family weren't helping him. They were a footballing family – his brother Bill had played for Middlesbrough – and they knew the problems. I thought they should have encouraged him to return. I told him: 'If this is all the game means to you, then you'd better carry on potato-picking.' He asked if he could have a transfer. 'I know a club up here that wants me,' he said.

'No one has spoken to me,' I said. 'In any case, who would want a player who walks out on his club?' Cliff Lloyd, who was secretary of the Professional Footballers' Association, spoke to him and eventually he returned to the club. Soon afterwards he got into the first team and has been a regular more or less ever since.

His attitude improved so much that he won a place in the England team. We discovered his best position – just behind the front strikers, where his ability to receive the ball, turn and take on defenders could be used to maximum effect.

Only Kevin Keegan is better than Gates at taking a pass under pressure and using it profitably. Eric was simply short of confidence and needed reassurance. I was able to give it to him when Alan Mullery, who was then manager of Brighton, rang one day to suggest a Peter Ward–Eric Gates swap. At the time Ward was a First Division regular and was being talked about as an England player.

I spoke to Gates and told him I wanted him to stay. 'How good do you think Ward is?' I asked him. 'Very good,' he replied. 'Well, that's how highly I rate you,' I said. 'I think you're a better player.' After that, his career began to take shape. He played brilliantly for long spells.

Gates was unlucky that his England opportunities were so limited. In his first match, against Norway, I thought he was used too deep. In the second, in Rumania, he ruined his chances by doing a silly thing. The day before the match he had stomach trouble and spent the day in bed. Next day, when Ron Greenwood asked him if he was fit to play, he said Yes. He quite clearly wasn't, however, and had to come off at half-time. It is difficult for a player who desperately wants to play for his country to admit that he isn't right, but he has to do it, for his own sake and for the sake of his team.

John Wark did that to me once, and I had to reprimand him severely. The match was against Manchester City and he had been injured. Before I picked the side he said he was fit to play, but once the game began I realised he wasn't. 'Never do that again,' I told him. 'You're cheating yourself, the club and me.'

The reason we were able to recruit players like Gates, Wark, Brazil, Burley, Butcher and Osman was that we spent more time than most clubs on the youth policy. We drove more miles than most managers and scouts. We had more late nights. I reorganised the scouting system and insisted that the scouts had club cars. Reg Tyrrell, who was chief scout when I arrived, used to drive around in an old banger. I made sure that Ron Gray, the present chief scout, had a new car. I travelled thousands of miles a year myself along with my assistant, Bobby Ferguson, Cyril Lea, Ron Gray or Charlie Woods to watch the most obscure matches, often arriving home at two or three in the morning. I still do it, and so do all my staff.

I have never seen Manchester United v. Manchester City or Liverpool v. Everton or Spurs v. Arsenal. The big city matches were not for me. I was never going to see a likely player appearing for those clubs. I attended Third and Fourth Division matches, youth matches or Central League games, often anonymously in a cap to avoid being detected. Nowadays it is almost impossible for me to go to a club without being noticed, so I usually make sure I see a game in comfort and sit in the directors' box.

One of the signings in my early days which gave me immense satisfaction was the arrival of Jimmy Robertson from Arsenal in March 1970. Ipswich were in relegation trouble and I bought Jimmy from Arsenal for £50,000 and Frank Clarke from QPR for a similar amount. They helped keep us in the First Division. Jimmy didn't want to come. Going from Highbury to Portman Road was a come-down for him, and he only signed because I promised I wouldn't prevent him moving on when he felt like it. He was a player who liked picking up his five per cent from frequent moves. He was with us just over two years before I sold him to Stoke for £80,000 – a profit of £30,000. Sound business!

Bryan Hamilton was another 'steal' of a signing. We bought him for £18,000 and he gave us five years' service before he was sold for £40,000. He was a lovely lad. Colin Viljoen, signed by McGarry from Johannesburg, cost the club nothing and eventually went for £100,000. Colin was one of the few players we had at the club during this period who was capped by England. He played twice for Don Revie in 1975 and became a naturalised British subject.

Ipswich was a team of hard workers at this time. We didn't have any stars, but Colin felt he had to be treated as one. Once when he went home to South Africa and said he wasn't coming back because he was dissatisfied with the new contract we had offered him. John Cobbold told me that this had happened before and that McGarry had flown out to South Africa to negotiate with him.

I decided to treat it differently. I sent him a cable saying: 'I can't negotiate with you six thousand miles away. Come back.' There was no reply, but not long afterwards a friend said he saw him in Ipswich. Colin's wife was English, and I knew he would stay with us. I had him in and he agreed to sign a new contract. It wasn't much different to the contracts I had negotiated with the other players. I didn't want to embarrass any of them. I had to be fair to everyone. Dealing with players who want more money is just one of the many problems faced by a manager.

As their playing careers are so short, the players want to squeeze the clubs for as much as they can get, but they have to be realistic. If the money isn't there, the club can't pay it. Colin wasn't a bad lad, really. He was a good player, sharp as a needle in his prime and a quick little passer. He made goals but didn't score many. Most of his problems came through injuries. He was a bit of a hypochondriac, as some players can be, and his later months with us were mainly spent in the treatment room. With John Wark and Brian Talbot coming through, I knew we could afford to release him and QPR were the first club interested.

I agreed terms at £100,000 with Rangers but the deal fell through when the QPR doctor found that one of his calfs was thinner than the other one. Colin had had Achilles tendon trouble and the doctor thought the calf problem was related to the injury. So QPR withdrew and Manchester City came in. Their doctor found nothing wrong with his calf.

One of my best signings was David Johnson from Everton in 1972. I heard he might be available and watched him four times before making my mind up. He was very quick, had a good right foot and finished well. He was rather scatter-brained as a person, though, and when I eventually signed him I used to call him Scatter Brain.

The story of how I landed him was very funny. Ipswich played a 2–2 draw at Goodison and after the match Harry Catterick, Everton's manager, said: 'Would you sell the big fella?' In football, anyone over a certain height is 'the big fella' and I thought he meant Allan Hunter.

'Oh no,' I said. 'We can't sell him. He was great today. If we got rid of him our defence would be full of holes.'

Catterick realised I was talking about a defender. 'No, I mean the lad up front, Belfitt,' he said. My heart jumped. We had paid Leeds £55,000 for Rod Belfitt and he was an average, bustling player. A good type, but not in Johnson's class.

'Well,' I said, 'we might be prepared to talk. Give me the weekend to think about it.' Then I added: 'But I'd like Johnson. What about letting me have him? He's not in your first team, whereas Belfitt is in mine!'

Catterick was keen. 'All right,' he said. 'We'll speak on Monday. Keep it quiet!' I certainly did! Sunday morning I was round at Belfitt's house soon after breakfast. He lived only four hundred yards from my home at the time. 'Everton want you,' I said. 'It's up to you what you decide. Have a think about it.'

On Monday before training he came to me and said his wife wasn't averse to the idea and he was willing to move to Merseyside.

Overjoyed, I rang Catterick and he said: 'That's fine, but I can't let you have a straight swap. We'd want some money as well.'

I offered him £40,000 and he accepted straight away. Belfitt went up to see him and signed after half an hour. It took me all day, however, to persuade Johnson to come to Ipswich. He was twenty-one, a single lad with no ties, but his roots were in Liverpool and it was a hard job to persuade him that he could advance his career by joining a small town club like Ipswich. Finally, he agreed to my terms and he went on to score thirty-five League goals for us in 137 League matches. He played eight times for England and both of us were happy. In 1976 I sold him to Liverpool for £200,000, so we made another profit and I was able to buy Paul Mariner from Plymouth, who was to succeed Johnson in the England team.

Johnson couldn't play for us in the FA Cup semi-final in 1975 and losing that game cost us the chance of doing the Double that season. He was injured in the four-game epic with Leeds in the sixth round, which ended when we won the third replay 3–2 at Leicester to earn the right to meet West Ham in the semi-final at Villa Park. Perhaps it might have ended differently had he been fit.

I remain convinced that we were robbed by FIFA referee Clive Thomas in the replay at Stamford Bridge after drawing at Villa Park. We lost 2–1, but had two perfectly good goals disallowed for off-side by Thomas. We have a film of the match on video and the evidence is clear-cut. Neither Bryan Hamilton nor Trevor Whymark was off-side, yet Mr Thomas said they were, and his verdicts were the ones that counted. He has often said to me since that he slipped up and I think he became a better referee for it.

Our chances were ruined when George Burley and Kevin Beattie were injured, and we lost in the most galling of circumstances. Whymark had to play at centre-half and Beattie went to centre-forward. Poor Burley couldn't come off, and he played through the second half with an ankle twice its normal size. We had the kind of bad luck in that game that Leeds used to experience under Revie in the seventies.

I rated Leeds at that time as one of the finest sides produced in this country. They had great players like Bremner, Giles, Charlton, Reaney, Madeley, Clarke and Eddie Gray, and they played marvellous football. They won trophies, but not as many as their football deserved. I know Revie was a very superstitious man, and the longer he was at Elland Road the worse his phobias got, but I do not consider that a factor in explaining the mystery of why his team so often failed when it should have succeeded.

Looking back over the outstanding club sides in England in the past thirty years, I suppose Leeds have to be ranked up alongside the Manchester United side that was partially destroyed at Munich, the Manchester United side of the late sixties which boasted George Best, Bobby Charlton and Denis Law, the Liverpool side of the seventies, the Arsenal Double-winning side, and the Spurs side of the early sixties which also did the Double.

In my formative years I spent a lot of time on the White Hart Lane terraces watching that great Spurs side of Danny Blanchflower, Dave Mackay, Jimmy Greaves and Bobby Smith. The players worked together so well. Smith was the ideal foil for Greaves. Blanchflower complemented Mackay. The blend was sensational, and that in my view is one of the basic ingredients of the truly great side: blend. You can have good players, but they won't necessarily make a good side unless they fit each other like pieces of a jigsaw.

I used to get off the bus at Seven Sisters and practically run to White Hart Lane. The atmosphere at the ground almost dragged you there. It was like a powerful stimulant. To me, there was no thrill in football to match it. I was there the night they outclassed Gornik in the European Cup after losing in Poland. What a night that was!

Would that Spurs side have been as successful in today's conditions? I think so. Of course the game is more compacted now. There is less space because the play is frequently pressed into a narrow strip in the centre of the pitch, but I am sure those fine players would have adapted. They would still be able to move the ball forward with accuracy and create chances for those sharp-shooters Greaves, Smith and Cliff Jones. They were so good at using the width of the pitch, so economical in their passes.

Arsenal's Double-winning side of 1971 cannot be discounted, but they lacked the artistry of Spurs and they failed to stay at the top very long. Liverpool under Bill Shankly and later Bob Paisley have shown us the virtues of teamwork and good habits, and Liverpool's performances have excited me nearly as much as those of Tottenham in those glory, glory days. Shankly was the motivator, the man who got response from his players by the way he said things. He would come in and say: 'By Christ!' And he would have their attention immediately. But he was also a good judge of a player.

Kevin Keegan is the prime example of this, and I must confess a personal interest. Like many managers at the time, I knew that Keegan, who was then at Scunthorpe, was available. I went to see him play on four separate occasions and each time I came to the same conclusion: he would find it difficult making the grade in the First Division!

When Shankly paid £33,000 for him I thought he was crazy. It was a large sum of money for a little lad who I didn't think had a chance of making it. The only thing in its favour was that Liverpool could afford to lose the money – they always spend their profits on new players instead of paying it in Corporation Tax – and it was no big loss for them. Keegan was struggling in the reserves until one day Shankly told him to play centre-forward in a practice match, and he was a revelation. From that moment on, Keegan went one way – upwards.

Liverpool's decision to promote Bob Paisley when Shankly retired was an inspired one. It saved them going through the trauma experienced at Elland Road when Don Revie left Leeds to take over as England manager. Brian Clough, Revie's successor, wanted to change things, as most new managers do, but there are some clubs you can't change overnight – and Liverpool and Leeds are two of them.

Paisley is a wily, level-headed person who is consistent in everything he does. I cannot see him retiring prematurely as Shankly did. Everyone has a Shankly story, and my favourite is about the time Shanks wanted to keep Tony Hateley on in a game and Paisley, then the trainer, wanted to take him off because he was playing so badly.

Hateley was a rare instance of Shankly misjudging the qualities of a player. He was good in the air but his control on the ground wasn't up to Liverpool's high standards, and his purchase had to be classed as one of Shankly's few mistakes. Anyway, in this particular game every time Paisley, who was sitting on the bench, turned towards Shankly to seek permission to substitute the struggling Hateley, Shankly turned away.

Finally, Hateley was felled in a collision with the centre-half and Paisley went on to treat him. Paisley took one look at the 'injury' and called for a stretcher. 'What's wrong?' asked an alarmed Hateley. 'Don't worry, son,' said Paisley. 'You're all right. We will look after you.'

Hateley was slightly stunned in the collision and must have been surprised to find that his legs had been taped together and he was being lifted gently on to the stretcher. 'Here, what's going on?' he said. 'Don't worry,' said Paisley. 'Leave it to us. Just sit back.'

Hateley was stretchered off, and on came the substitute. Shankly came down to see what was wrong with Hateley. 'How is he?' Shankly asked. 'I'm just making sure that now we've got him off you're not going to get him back on again,' explained Paisley.

The two successful sides created by Matt Busby relied on the quality of the players Busby collected around him. They weren't teams whose victories came from any tactical plans or from coaching. The players just went out and played. When you have players like Duncan Edwards, Tommy Taylor, Roger Byrne, Eddie Colman, Bobby Charlton, George Best and Denis Law it is easy to do that. Everyone wishes he had players of that calibre!

George Best was the greatest of the lot, the greatest player I have seen in my time in the game. He had spontaneous natural ability that could tear a game inside out. He wasn't just an artist who could perform amazing dribbling tricks and score phenomenal goals. He was also an all-round player who was brave and could tackle as hard as any defender.

What happened to him was a tragedy, and like most managers, I sometimes wonder if Best would have become an alcoholic if he had been under me at Portman Road. If he had been, I do not feel his career would have turned out any differently. Manchester United tried everything but failed. He was the victim of his own easy-going temperament and the hangers-on he attracted. The pressures were too much for him.

I had a better idea than most people in Soccer about what the name George Best meant to football and society generally, because Ipswich played at Old Trafford the week the final break came and we were discussing it in the boardroom afterwards.

Someone said George's agent was outside, panicking because George had disappeared. The agent was shown in. 'You've got to do something,' he said. 'I've got this pile of contracts here and they're useless without him.'

He put the contracts on the table. The amounts totalled £500,000! These days that would be worth about £1.5 million. Matt Busby shook his head. 'There's nothing more we can do,' he said. 'We've tried everything.'

Best wasn't the first player to be ruined by drink. I see booze as one of the major evils in the game. And its influence has become more widespread now there is big money to be earned. In my day it was half a lager. Today they're drinking spirits. These players reach the top and forget the hard work they have put in to get there. They ignore the fact that to stay at the top, you have to work even harder.

They squander their riches and all the accountants, bank managers, investment managers and agents cannot save them from themselves. This life of luxury doesn't last forever, but some players think it does. One player whose career might have taken him to the heights of the game if he had been more disciplined was Alan Hudson, formerly of Chelsea, Stoke and Arsenal. I was a victim of his skill early in my managerial career when he was credited with a 'goal' at Stamford Bridge which went into the side netting. Referee Roy Capey was about the only person present who thought the ball went into the net.

Hudson was a precocious, audacious player who was majestic on the ball. There was nothing he couldn't do and he had it in him to lift himself into the Mannion–Shackleton class. But he ruined his chances because he drank too much and didn't have enough rest. No athlete, however fit, can indulge himself and expect a long career at the top. You don't see many top golfers living it up. They are the most dedicated of sportsmen, and that is why they remain high in the rankings so long.

I saw Hudson when I was in Tampa in 1978 and seeing him reminded me of what a talent England had lost. He was bare-footed and wearing dirty jeans, and though it was mid-afternoon, he had been drinking heavily. It made me sad.

Nine

Every Man for Himself!

The pounding on the dressing-room door was so loud, so incessant, that I thought the door was about to give way. In the corner of the room was a crate full of lemonade bottles. I pointed at the bottles and said to the players: 'Take one each. If they get in here, make sure you don't miss. It's every man for himself.'

Allan Hunter, typical of him, wanted to unlock the door and take them on but I had no intention of letting that happen. We had just qualified for the third round of the UEFA Cup in the Olympic Stadium, Rome, in our second match in Europe. The date was 7 November 1973. We had survived on a 6–4 aggregate and outside were players of the losing Lazio side, furious and vengeful at having lost.

They were more like demented animals, a pack of wolves, than a group of human beings. For the first time in my years in football I felt fear for my safety and the safety of my players. It was the worst moment of my life. If that door had been broken down, I dread to think what the outcome would have been. There were no police on duty. No security. It was them against us, and fortunately the door stood firm.

No sooner had the referee sounded the final whistle and we had started to leave the pitch than some of the Italians began chasing us and aiming blows. I rushed on to the pitch to protect David Johnson, who scored the goal near the end which settled it. 'Come on,' I shouted. 'Let's get out of here!'

As we sprinted across the running track used in the 1960 Olympic Games, the Lazio players ran after us. There was a pitched battle as we struggled to go up the steps to the dressing-rooms. Hunter was in the middle of it and David Best, our goalkeeper, was kicked and hacked by Guiseppe Wilson, the Lazio defender.

The Italians were screaming and cursing as they tried to rain blows on the half-dozen of us who brought up the rear. Hunter wanted to trade blow for blow but I shouted: 'Let's get out of here. Get in that dressing-room.'

There is a time when it is braver to run away and this was one of them. I knew we could be in trouble if we stayed and turned it into a pitched battle. I realised what the repercussions would be: we would be banned from Europe along with Lazio. I had to protect the name of the club. Reaching the sanctuary of the dressing-room, we slammed and bolted the door. A few more minutes went by before the banging and the shouting died away. It was like a scene from a madhouse. I had not come across anything like it – nor do I want to again.

It was quite a while before we ventured out of that dressing-room. Colin Harper, my full-back, sat in a corner nursing a knee injury which was to end his career. Hunter, defiant as ever, was rallying the troops. The rest sat there shocked and angry that something like this could happen to them.

When I emerged some time later, the Italian Press were waiting to talk to me about the game. 'Never mind the game,' I said with deep feeling. 'What about the fighting afterwards when your players set on my team? What is your club going to do about that? What is your President going to do?' They stood sheepishly and said nothing. They knew the conduct of the Lazio players was indefensible.

Some of our fans were also attacked as they left the stadium. Anyone speaking English was set upon. Our supporters had to hide their scarves and rosettes. Two hours elapsed before the police, who at last showed up, said it was safe for us to drive off in the team coach. The players squatted under the seats, fearful that bricks would be hurled through the windows.

We didn't go back to the hotel because we had been advised that five thousand incensed Lazio supporters were waiting for us. Instead we drove to the mountains and found a quiet restaurant where we had a late meal. We stayed there until 3.30, when it was decided that it would be safe to return to our hotel.

I was warned in advance that there would be trouble in Lazio. Bertie Mee, manager of Arsenal, rang me and said: 'You can be involved in a war over there. Their players will spit and poke fingers in the eyes of your players. They will be up to every trick. Your players need to show the utmost discipline.'

Lazio didn't need to resort to such tactics because they were a good side with some good players. We beat them 4–0 in the first leg at Portman Road, chiefly through a brilliant performance from Trevor Whymark, who scored all four goals. Georgio Chinaglia, who became one of the most successful players ever to take part in the North American Soccer League, was with them at the time and he was big and strong – not too skilful, but a considerable opponent. It was no surprise to me that he became a star in America, where standards are lower.

A foretaste of what we could expect in Rome came when David Johnson was kicked in the testicles, quite deliberately in my opinion. It was an appalling injury. As we helped him off, blood was everywhere. He needed a lot of stitching in his scrotum and his penis, and for days afterwards couldn't walk properly.

A few days later Johnson was at the club when some of the directors were in the boardroom. He came in and John Cobbold asked him how the injury was progressing. 'Here,' said Johnson, unzipping his trousers, 'have a look for yourselves.'

'Goodness me,' said Mr John. 'Put that thing away!' Harold Smith, one of the directors, said: 'What you need is a transplant!'

'Not from one of you buggers,' said Johnson. Everyone was roaring with laughter. That typifies the spirit at Ipswich Football Club. Though we pride ourselves on being professional, it is a fun club and not much time elapses without a joke being cracked or someone laughing.

I cannot imagine the Johnson boardroom incident taking place at many other clubs. But John and Patrick Cobbold have encouraged a light-hearted atmosphere off the field, and I think other clubs like coming to Ipswich for that reason.

My own relationship with the Cobbolds has always been a fairly jovial one. I remember we were waiting at Barbados airport one balmy day for our plane to arrive from Trinidad. A Pan-Am jet was coming into land and I said: 'I wonder where that plane has come from?' 'From the sky, you dolthead,' was Mr Patrick's reply.

Often their humour rebounds on them. When we played in Innsbruck four players, including Paul Mariner, broke the curfew and had to be reprimanded. Next day the Ipswich directors were entertained by their Innsbruck counterparts, and Rudolph Samms, the Innsbruck director who was also chief of police, said to Patrick: 'We have arrested Paul Mariner after last night's incident.'

Patrick looked concerned. 'But don't worry,' added Samms, 'we will release him after the match!'

Johnson, Mariner's predecessor in the team, was a very brave player and though not fully recovered after his brutal injury against Lazio, insisted on coming with us to Rome for the second leg. The stadium wasn't quite full when we arrived but the atmosphere was extremely intimidating.

This was my first experience of Italian football and I didn't like it. There were sinister undertones throughout our stay. The day before the match, officials of Roma, Lazio's rival club, presented Whymark with a statuette in commemoration of his feat in scoring all four goals in the first leg. When photographs appeared of the presentation the next day, the Lazio fans were angry. I do not know whether Roma meant it as an insulting gesture to their rivals. At the time, I didn't think so, but it may have been.

Anyway, it didn't help cool the explosive atmosphere at the stadium. Lazio attacked from the start and put us under enormous pressure. They scored one goal, then two, then three, so the aggregate score was 4–3 to us. A British flag was torn from its pole and burnt. Just as Bertie Mee said they would, the Italians spat at my players and tried to provoke them with unfair tactics at every opportunity.

But the worst scenes came when Clive Woods was hacked down and the Dutch referee Leonardus van der Kroft awarded a penalty. An Italian grabbed the ball and kicked it into the crowd. Another Italian squared up to Colin Viljoen, who was preparing to take the spot kick. When the ball was eventually returned and placed on the spot, a Lazio player kicked it away.

By now the Dutch referee had lost control. He should have started cautioning players and sending them off, but he took no action.

At last the ball was in position and Viljoen was able to take the kick. Happily, he scored to make the aggregate 5–3 in our favour. One of the Italians chased after him, trying to strike him and Viljoen had to keep running to avoid him. As the referee blew for the restart, the Italian was in our half, still pursuing Viljoen!

We had already lost Harper with a knee injury, and now it was becoming apparent that I would have to put on another substitute as Woods was being subjected to frightening intimidation. Defenders went after him irrespective of whether or not he had the ball, accusing him of diving and attempting to molest him. Woods was white in the face.

There were seventeen minutes remaining and Johnson, sitting next to me on the bench, said: 'I'll go on.' I said: 'Are you sure?' He hadn't recovered from his horrendous injuries from two weeks before but he replied: 'Yes, I'm sure I'm sure.' I put him on for Woods and he ran through the middle to score our second goal – cancelling out another one scored by Lazio. We lost 4–2 on the night but qualified 6–4 on aggregate.

Before Johnson went on, a Lazio substitute, pretending to warm up, spat all over me as he ran past. There were so many incidents happening on the pitch that I just shrugged it off. But it was typical of the club and its players at that time.

On our return, we wrote to UEFA calling for disciplinary action to be taken. It was. Lazio were banned from Europe for a year and fined £1,000. I thought it was a ridiculously lenient punishment, especially as we had been fined £400 that season when a Polish referee Janusz Eksztajn alleged that he had been struck by a missile fired from a catapult in the home leg of our first-round tie against Real Madrid.

Our club doctor found no evidence of injury but the referee claimed that he felt a sharp pain. The doctor said it was probably a minor muscle tear or an accidental kick. We were so annoyed that we decided to appeal, and David Rose, the club secretary, and one of the directors attended an appeal in Zurich only to learn that the original fine was increased!

Ipswich have been punished twice by UEFA, both times rather unjustly in my view. The second occasion was in November 1978, when a fine of £1,200 was imposed following incidents in the second leg of a European Cup Winners' Cup tie in Innsbruck, Austria. UEFA didn't contact us for our version of what happened and the first we knew of it was when a telegram was received at Portman Road saying we had been fined and Paul Mariner suspended for two matches.

The Innsbruck trip was an eventful one for us in a number of ways. The problems began on the first night with the drinking incident when four senior players broke the curfew. I looked on it as a serious breach of discipline, and fined the players two hundred pounds each. But all four took their punishment like men and played magnificently two nights later.

Ipswich won the first leg 1–0, and I foresaw that the second match in a packed, cramped stadium under the mountains would be a high-pressure occasion, and that was how it turned out. There was so much noise that the players couldn't hear me as I shouted instructions, and I believed Mariner when he said he didn't hear the whistle go for off-side in extra time as he ran on and put the ball in the net. He had been previously cautioned for dissent so the Polish referee Alojzy Jarguz sent him off for committing a second offence, namely time-wasting.

Five more of my players were cautioned, John Wark, Mick Mills, David Geddis, Les Tibbott and Eric Gates, and we conceded thirty-three free kicks in a rugged match. But the worst incident went unpunished by the referee – a scything tackle on George Burley by the Innsbruck captain Peter Koncilia right in front of the bench. It looked to be an attempt to break George's leg and I jumped to my feet in rage.

George Burley is a fine advertisement for the profession and I was upset to see him assaulted in such a ruthless fashion. Everyone else on the bench jumped up with me, while Geddis, who had been substituted, tried to remonstrate with Koncilia, only to be punched. An Innsbruck official pushed one of the Ipswich reserves violently in the chest. It was fitting that George Burley should score the goal in the hundredth minute which gave us a quarter-final tie against Barcelona.

We were to go out on the away goal rule in front of 100,000 fans in the Camp Nou Stadium, the second time our European hopes had ended in Barcelona. There was no argument on that occasion. We lost to a better side, but in a UEFA Cup third round match in November 1977 I refused to accept that that was the case. I felt we were very badly treated. There have been cases where referees have been bribed, and after our experience in Barcelona that thought fleetingly crossed my mind. Every decision went against us and I found it hard to accept that it was all down to bad luck.

The first leg was uneventful. We won 3–0 and Roger Osborne did a superb marking job on the legendary Dutchman Johan Cruyff. Roger was a very basic player who nearly always played to his maximum. Cruyff never got going and showed little inclination to do much about it.

He appeared to be past his prime. When he was in his heyday I rated him one of the best players of modern times – a quick, skilful player who was capable of controlling a game as he demonstrated in Holland's 2–0 victory over England at Wembley in 1977. I had a brief chat with him and thought he was a very nice, unaffected person.

In the second match in Barcelona, he was a different player. Osborne was torn to pieces and Barcelona won 3–0, qualifying for the next round on penalties. That penalty shoot-out ought not to have been necessary, because I thought the Austrian referee Erich Linemayr made some totally unfair decisions during the match, all against Ipswich.

The first was when Barcelona had a corner, and with twenty-one players in the box – too many from Barcelona's viewpoint, because the more men there are in the area, the less chance there is of a goal – we succeeded in knocking the ball away, as we thought, to safety, with only two minutes remaining. But a Barcelona player was lying on the ground and the referee awarded a penalty. My players asked who had fouled. No one had committed an offence. The fellow went down on his own and the referee fell for it. Rexias scored and put the aggregate level at 3–3.

The second incident was when Paul Mariner went in on a through ball and despite having his shirt pulled, succeeded in going on and beating the goalkeeper. The referee called play back and gave us a free kick for the foul on Paul – a scandalous decision. Later on, Geddis was flattened in the area and no penalty was awarded.

Both teams usually give the referee and linesmen souvenirs or mementos after matches, and this was one night when I felt like withholding our present. But David Rose took the gifts in. I rarely want to go in to see a referee after a match, but I was so depressed and angry that I did so on this occasion. I wanted to ask him who had fouled for the Barcelona penalty and why he had called Mariner back. The UEFA observer was in the room at the time and ordered me out. He said he would report me if I persisted.

He was right. Nothing is ever gained from arguing with a referee afterwards. He is not going to change the result. It was a bitter experience for me and I was so emotionally involved that I found it impossible to sleep that night. These European matches bring an extra stress because you are fighting for your country and there is more attention focused on you from television, radio and the news-papers.

But I enjoy them nevertheless. They represent a welcome break from the normal routine. It is a chance to travel, a chance to meet new people and an opportunity to improve one's knowledge of foreign football. In nine out of the last ten years, Ipswich were in Europe, and that was a factor in keeping me at the club. We became known throughout Europe and were respected as a good footballing side.

There are disadvantages of course. Often when a club has

travelled back on the Thursday and face an away match on the Saturday the performance of the players suffers. Playing too many matches in Europe could even cost a club the League title, and I believe that may have happened to us in 1980–1. Don Howe once said it's a good thing to have a year out of Europe – and he is right – but I would still miss the excitement of competing against the best club sides in Europe.

Ipswich started right at the top when we played our first match under my leadership in 1973. We were drawn against the Spanish champions Real Madrid who, though not the power they had been in the days of di Stefano and Puskas, were still a very good side. The critics gave us no chance, but we surprised them by winning 1–0 at home and holding Real to a 0–0 draw in front of 80,000 fans in the Bernabeu Stadium.

Our showing in Spain was as brave and forthright a performance as I have ever seen from a British club. Real's side was full of internationals, including the West German World Cup star Gunter Netzer who was less influential than I feared he might be. That result established our reputation abroad. The big clubs now knew we were a club to be respected.

Clubs can make a lot of money from being involved in European competitions, and I have always maintained that the players deserve a share of it. In addition to their normal bonuses and appearance money, we have a system at Ipswich whereby the players share twenty per cent of the profit from any European cup competition. Playing in Europe makes them better players and it demands higher standards.

Hostile crowds can make or break a player, and I can claim that most of mine came through these experiences with credit and emerged as better players. I remember a night in Leipzig in 1974 when we lost on penalties in the UEFA Cup. There were 70,000 fans in the stadium, and every time one of their players took a penalty, there was complete silence. When one of ours did so, the noise was like a crescendo, with everyone whistling shrilly. We lost when Hunter missed a penalty, which was rank injustice because he had given one of the greatest centre-half displays I had seen.

Mick Mills was sent off after only ten minutes and with ten men we managed to hold the East Germans to a one-goal lead. It was so tense sitting on the bench that Bryan Hamilton, who never smoked in his life before that moment, was chain smoking and didn't realise he was doing it.

It was a memorable, gutsy performance and I said to the directors afterwards: 'Some of our players aged five years tonight but they will be better players for it.'

Normally I fine players who are sent off but I took no action this time in the case of Mills because I considered that he had been fouled first and had retaliated. He had suffered enough in being sent off.

A performance to match the one in Madrid was in Las Palmas in 1977 when we drew 3–3 after winning 1–0 at home. The spirit shown that night in the face of a bellicose, noisy, missile-throwing crowd was quite outstanding.

Two years earlier we threw away a 3–0 advantage when we lost 4–0 to the tough Belgian side Bruges in the UEFA Cup. That was a shattering night. One of the lows in my European career. But in the main our forays into Europe have been enjoyable, satisfying experiences and one thing which is to the credit of Ipswich Town Football Club is that in nine years there was not one instance of crowd trouble initiated by our fans. The record of our supporters has been exemplary. And the same can be said, generally speaking, about the players.

Ten

'*Turn the Flame-Throwers on Them!*'

On the night of 11 March 1978 I was sitting in the lounge at home with Elsie watching *Match of the Day* on television. Jimmy Hill, my former Fulham team-mate, was introducing the programme and he referred to Ipswich Town's FA Cup tie at Millwall that day which had been interrupted by hooliganism.

Jimmy said there had been some strong words from Bobby Robson about the affair. He quoted me as saying: 'These people are killing football ... I would turn the flame-throwers on them.'

Elsie went pale. 'You didn't say that, did you?' she said. I felt sick to the pit of my stomach. 'Well no,' I said. 'Not for public consumption. They've got hold of something I said in private.' I was very angry. I went to the telephone and dialled the BBC's number. I managed to reach John Motson, who is a friend, and he was reluctant to give me Jimmy Hill's number. Eventually I persuaded him to tell me and next morning I rang Hill.

'You quoted me last night about flame-throwers and I didn't say that,' I said. 'You could have checked it with me first. You owed that to me. Who told you?'

'We got it from a good authority,' he said. 'You know my number,' I said. 'You've rung me enough times. I'm always available. I always try to help.'

He gave the impression there was little he could do about it. The damage had been done. Fortunately for my peace of mind someone from the Jimmy Young Radio Two programme called me later and asked me to appear on Jimmy Young's show the next morning to talk about the subject of hooliganism, which gave me a chance to put the record straight. I didn't want to be known as the man who advocated burning football hooligans to death!

What happened at Millwall were the worst scenes I have witnessed at a football match. Some louts starting hurling bricks and other missiles at our supporters at the far end of the stand, and some of the injuries were horrendous. The referee ordered the players back to the dressing-rooms for eighteen minutes while police quelled the disturbance, and I left my seat in the directors' box to walk behind the stand to the dressing-rooms. I recognised some of the victims and I saw how terrified they were. I felt a terrible shame that I could be associated with a game which produced horrors on this scale. Of course it wasn't football's fault, but it was there in our game and it made me wonder what more we could have done to prevent not just this outbreak, but hundreds of others every season.

The police had under-estimated the threat from the mobs who were associated with Millwall at that time – the so-called 'F Troop', 'Halfway Line' and 'The Treatment', all gangs of nasty people who had been glamorised in the BBC programme *Panorama*. There was inadequate segregation and this contributed to the trouble. Later that month the FA found Millwall guilty and ordered them to close their ground for two matches and fined them £1,500. The club was instructed to carry out certain safety precautions and was banned from staging a home FA Cup tie for two years. I felt sorry for Millwall. Their directors apologised at the time but it was something they had no power over. For some reason the big city clubs attract hooligans and their actions disfigure our national game.

Hooliganism is virtually unknown among Ipswich fans. Living in a quiet rural area, our fans don't fight and it came as a frightful shock that day when the Millwall people attacked them. UEFA officials have said many times that the record of Ipswich fans abroad is one of the best in Europe, and on the rare occasions when we have disturbances at Portman Road the trouble is caused by visiting fans.

I had friends who were hit by bricks at the Den, and I sympathised with their anger and rage at the time. I was as upset as they were and I remember having several conversations about what should be done. Somebody said: 'It's a pity we can't machine-gun them.'

After our 6–1 victory and the usual Press conference, I was discussing the matter with some people in the directors' lounge and a number of similar remarks were made. It was then that I said: 'We should turn the flame-throwers on them' – or words to that effect. It was a figure of speech. Like when a forward misses an open goal, and a manager says: 'He should be shot for that.' I wasn't seriously suggesting that flame-throwers should be used. . . .

But there must have been a few reporters within earshot, because I understand these quotes were relayed to the newspaper, radio and television offices. It proved to be one of the most embarrassing moments of my life. I received a heavier than normal mail over the next few days, most of it supporting my views. Several ex-Army people were very enthusiastic in their support, but I did receive some other letters saying I was a sadist.

I fear it is true that football administrators and clubs generally did not act soon enough to curb hooliganism. In the early days there was a feeling that if it was left alone it would go away quietly like the Margate mods against rockers disturbances and other teenage crazes. But it didn't disappear. It mushroomed to such an extent that I believe it threatened the future of our national game.

If action hadn't been taken, I think the situation would have become terminal. But the right measures were introduced just before we started slipping over the brink of the precipice. The magistrates' courts, which had previously been too lenient, began to recognise that football hooliganism had wider ramifications, and penalties were increased. Youths were sent away to centres for a short dose of shock treatment.

The police were allowed to go in among the troublemakers and sort them out. They had been held back previously and it wasn't working. A more aggressive response has enabled the police to root out the ring-leaders and abort much of their mischief. On the Continent police are much more aggressive than they are here, and generally I support that. If hooligans know they are going to be punished they are less likely to start trouble.

There is the argument that aggression breeds aggression and that it is the last thing you want, but since the sixties football hooliganism has worsened under the soft approach, whereas now that there has been a tougher reaction to it, the figures have declined, so there must be a case for sterner policing methods.

Segregation and fencing have reduced the incidence of disorders, and though I deplore that these innovations should be necessary, I recognise their value. I have the highest praise for the police at football matches.

They have a difficult task every Saturday both inside and outside grounds, yet they carry it out with dignity and considerable success. I believe they are winning the battle. Most clubs co-operate with police in seeing that visiting supporters are escorted to grounds and bussed out of town as soon as possible afterwards. Not so long ago, I think we reached a point in the game's history when a ban on away supporters was very close.

Most of the trouble inside grounds is caused when the away fans clash with the home fans, so if there were no away fans there would be fewer fights. Such a ban would have been difficult to enforce but it could have worked to a certain extent. Coach operators could have been barred from transporting large numbers of supporters and British Rail's cheap trips could also have been stopped.

All the trouble we have at Portman Road is caused at the Portman Walk end, part of which is reserved for away fans. We have police on the turnstiles there searching every fan for offensive weapons, yet still a vast amount of damage is caused each season. These people must have screw-drivers for fingers. Once when Manchester United played at Portman Road, damage totalled £1,500. It was unbelievable what those young people did to the steel stands and barriers.

In an incident at Norwich, Manchester United fans climbed on the roof and started stripping sheets of steel off it. One fan fell through the roof but was unhurt. It costs Ipswich around £1,500 a match for policing, and if you add up the figures spent by all the clubs it is a substantial amount going out of the game each Saturday.

It is an unnecessary expense because if fans were well behaved, as they were when I was a teenager at St James's Park, no squads of police would be needed. There is no easy answer to the problem, otherwise it would have been tried by now. It is a weekly battle, and luckily the police are winning.

All-seat stadiums are not the answer, because there has been fighting even at grounds where there are no terraces. Probably hooliganism would be reduced, but it wouldn't be eliminated. When there are only seats at a ground, people who prefer standing are penalised. I believe the terrace is still an integral part of our football.

If the away fan was discouraged, it would take away much of the atmosphere from grounds. The fervour and excitement of fans is a stimulus to the players and I wouldn't like to see matches played in front of rows of quiet customers. But as football has become more and more a business, the competitiveness of the fans has increased as much as that of the players.

There is a section of supporters who will follow a winning side. It used to be Leeds, then it was Liverpool, and it is always Manchester United. They come from all over the country and they identify with their club. I suppose it is something in their upbringing and their environment which produces this urge to be aggressive and abusive. Rivalry is no longer conducted on a sporting basis.

Gone are the amateur days. Now it is a highly explosive professional sport watched by a majority of people who insist on seeing their team win. I do not think the way the game is played today has encouraged hooliganism. Bad behaviour off the field is seldom a product of bad behaviour on the field.

In fact there is much less thuggery in football today than there was when I was starting out thirty years ago. There is less bad tackling and charging of opponents. The difference now is that there is more attention given in the newspapers, radio and television to such incidents. In my day, if you were fouled you got up and carried on playing, maybe hoping to square the account at a later opportunity. But today there is more retaliation. Most of the players cautioned these days are cautioned for 'having a go' back.

You never saw masses of players crowding round an incident, as sometimes happens now. There was little or no squaring up and arguing. Money must be the prime reason for this change in attitude. You wouldn't kick your grandmother for four pounds, but there must be players who would think hard about it for two hundred.

Crowds can sometimes react to controversial incidents. They don't like cheats, nor do they like play actors. I try to discourage players from going down unless they are genuinely injured. I tell them: 'When you are lying there, we're down to ten men and it could cost us a goal. You're a cheat!' These days referees tend to let games go on, because they know crowds don't like continual stoppages for trainers to come on to treat players.

We try to give young players a proper grounding at Ipswich in standards of behaviour. I think that is one of the reasons for our success, because players have come up through the system and know the standards we expect to be maintained. When a club buys a player, they can know little about his character, his personality, whether he mixes well, whether he is a trouble maker. A bought player represents a risk. A player who is developed through the system is no risk.

There are some malingerers and hypochondriacs in the game, but not many. Mick Mills is a good example of a hardy player who will only go down when he is really hurt. And one of the bravest acts I can remember was the performance of another of the game's longest-serving players, John Wile of West Bromwich Albion, in the semi-final of the FA Cup in 1978 after clashing heads with Brian Talbot.

Wile split his head open yet insisted on carrying on with a bandage round his head. The blood was flying everywhere and when Ron Atkinson brought him off in a tactical substitution he was furious, snatching the bandage and hurling it into the ground. Most clubs have their John Wiles. These are the players the fans should look up to and idolise, not the cheats and play actors.

Eleven

A Winner at Last

The only time I have experienced player power in my managerial career was the week before the FA Cup Final against Arsenal in 1978, and it gave me some disturbing moments. The players, who had always supported me, suddenly decided that they didn't agree with my selection of the side, and deliberately sought to change it. In the end they were right and in effect I had to bow to player power. But I don't believe in it and never will. The manager is responsible for choosing his team, and the ultimate decision must always be left with him. He can ask players for their advice but he can never allow them to say: 'We want so-and-so in,' or: 'We don't want so-and-so.'

We had several injuries before the 1978 final, and the week before I was thinking of recalling some of the injured players who were close to fitness. One of them was Colin Viljoen, one of my longest-serving players who had been out injured since February. He had been a class player and I owed it to him to give him the chance of proving that he could do a job in the Cup Final.

The match before the Cup Final was away to Aston Villa and I brought Viljoen into the centre of midfield and moved Brian Talbot to right-half in place of Roger Osborne, and John Wark to left-half where Talbot had been playing. Talbot didn't like it and rebelled. I told him he had to do what he was told and he was unhappy about it. I knew the other players didn't like Viljoen but I failed to sense how deep their resentment had become about his attitude, both in training and around the club.

We lost that match at Villa Park 6–1 and it was apparent from the way that some of the players performed that they weren't trying as hard as they could have done. They didn't respond to Viljoen and some were loath to give him the ball. They played without spirit. I was very angry afterwards. Because Paul Cooper wasn't quite ready we had to play an eighteen-year-old apprentice goalkeeper, Paul Overton – and he was our best player. He made some brilliant saves.

'But for him we would have lost by ten goals,' I told the players. 'That says a lot about you. Our best player is an eighteen-year-old kid making his début.'

I was powerless to take any disciplinary action. I couldn't drop any of them for the Cup Final, and they knew it. I could hardly bring in seven or eight new players for a match of that importance. Before the game I had been undecided about my Wembley line-up. Now, twenty minutes after the second biggest beating in my life – a 7–0 defeat against Sheffield United was the worst – I knew what I had to do.

I had to revert to a midfield of Talbot, Wark and Osborne, and leave Viljoen out. I made a mistake in recalling Viljoen at this stage of the season and told him so. He accepted my decision and claimed, quite rightly, that he had been the victim of player power. He didn't travel with the rest of the team to the Hertfordshire hotel where we spent Cup Final week, preferring to remain at Portman Road. Early in the week he told a newspaper reporter his version of what had happened, and it was unwelcome publicity for us in the most vital week of the club's recent history. But it had cleared the air. The internal squabble was over and I knew what my Wembley team would be. Hunter, still plagued by a knee injury, was in the side at Villa Park, but Beattie, who hadn't played for three weeks because of his long-standing knee trouble, wasn't. The only remaining doubt in my mind was whether Hunter and Beattie would be fit.

Trevor Whymark also played at Villa, though not match fit, and I knew he wasn't ready for a Cup Final. David Geddis, the twenty-year-old reserve from Carlisle who had been in and out of the side, would have to be the other striker along with Paul Mariner. Except for the worries about Hunter and Beattie, everything went in our favour. No one gave us a chance, so there was no pressure on us and the training went marvellously. The mental side of it, the factor that influences the outcome of so many Cup Finals, was in our favour. While Arsenal fretted we relaxed and enjoyed ourselves.

Bobby Ferguson, my assistant, watched Arsenal several times and said the main threat in their side was on the left where Alan Hudson, Liam Brady and Sammy Nelson performed little triangles and provided most of the passes for the front three of Alan Sunderland, Malcolm Macdonald and Frank Stapleton. I said: 'All right, let's keep our left side intact, where we are also strongest, and try to disrupt theirs by playing Geddis as a right-winger.'

Geddis had never played on the flank before but he had a great game, possibly the finest of his career. He stopped Nelson coming forward and did some outstanding things with the ball himself. And it was his cross into the area which Willie Young mishit to Roger Osborne in the seventy-seventh minute for Roger to score the only goal of the match. Playing Geddis wide meant that Mariner had to play on his own in the middle, but he is one of the few strikers in the country capable of doing that, and he too had an excellent match. When we lost possession, I told Mariner to take O'Leary and not bother about Young. O'Leary, as he showed early on, posed a threat when coming forward, but we reasoned that Willie's distribution wasn't in the same class and we could afford to let him have the ball.

Tactically, the match was a huge success for us. Clive Woods ran the legs off Pat Rice, Talbot ran himself silly, and Osborne followed Brady everywhere.

Brady wasn't fit, it is true, but Osborne still did a relentlessly effective job on him. Everyone in the club was delighted that Roger should score the goal, because he had been such a loyal clubman. He gave so much on a hot, humid day that he was overcome with exhaustion, and when half a dozen players jumped on him to offer their congratulations, he almost passed out. Cyril Lea, the trainer, took some time to revive him and all he could say was: 'I can't carry on.' I had told Cyril to make sure he kept going because the substitute, Micky Lambert, was a winger and we didn't want another winger on with only thirteen minutes to go.

Cyril came back and said: 'His legs have gone. He'll have to come off.' So I sent on Lambert and he played at right-half for the first time in his career. I suppose the substitute should have been Russell Osman, an eighteen-year-old who had played twenty-eight League games that season, because of the doubts about Hunter and Beattie. But I wanted to reward Lambert's loyalty. He had been with the club eleven years and it was his testimonial match the following Monday. By winning the Cup, we were able to swell the attendance for him and he banked £20,000.

Hunter's fitness had been in doubt until the morning of the match. The Press and TV interviews had gone well, and everything was perfect when we retired for the night on the eve of the match. In the early hours, however, we were awakened by the sound of the fire alarms going off. A former employee of the hotel had returned and was threatening the assistant manager with a knife. There had been a minor fire as well and the fire brigade arrived with the police. It was the last thing a Cup Final team needed on the night before the match! I got to sleep at last, but next morning was woken by another commotion.

Cyril Lea and Bobby Ferguson were banging at my door. 'Look boss,' they said. 'Hunter is out there testing his knee.' We had arranged to give Hunter a fitness test at eleven o'clock, but he hadn't been able to sleep and went out on the hotel lawn at 8.45 to give himself a private test. Normally the other players would be sleeping in but the noise woke them too and they were at their windows shouting encouragement to Hunter. 'The Big Man' was so keen to play that he couldn't wait for his test. He signalled that he was fit to play and there was a loud cheer from the players.

Early in the match he came across to take the ball off Macdonald in one of the most decisive moments of the game. It was a beautiful tackle. He took the ball, the man, the grass, everything. It served notice on Macdonald that he would be in for a rugged afternoon. We went on to dominate the match, striking the woodwork three times.

The odds of 5–2 were ridiculous in a two-team event, and at the pre-match lunch some of the players who were arranging for friends to put bets on for them asked me whether I'd like to put some money on too.

'All right,' I said, 'Shove twenty pounds on for me.' I thought it would show my confidence in the team. We all felt we would win. 'I can't see us losing,' I told them. When they went out of the room, they all believed it.

That was the Wembley game when an official asked Lady Blanche Cobbold, the Ipswich President, a dear old lady who has been associated with the club all her life, whether she would like to meet a guest, Mrs Margaret Thatcher. 'I'd much sooner have a gin and tonic,' said Lady Blanche. It was a dream of a day. The weather was superb and so was the behaviour of the two sets of fans. It was the first time for years that the crowd sang the words of 'God save the Queen' uninterrupted by chanting and abuse.

On the way home the next day to a wonderful reception the team coach, escorted by police outriders, stopped at the Army and Navy pub in Chelmsford for a lunchtime drink. We had used the Army and Navy for meals on previous FA Cup trips that season and wanted to record our thanks to the manager and staff. As Mr John

Cobbold said: 'It's the first time I have been shown into a pub for a drink by police.'

Don Howe, my friend from West Bromwich Albion days, was one of the first people to congratulate me. 'You were better than us,' he said. 'We're not ready yet. We're a young side and one or two of them aren't experienced enough.' Terry Neill, generous in defeat, said: 'Don't worry, we'll be back next year.' And they were!

There was to be a tragic ending to the story for David Geddis. The following season he went out to a disco with another young player, Peter Canavan, a six-foot centre-half from Ash Winning, and on their way home in the early hours his MGB hit a barrier at 70 m.p.h. and they were thrown through the canvas roof. The police said later they were hurtled nearly one hundred yards in the air, such was the force of the impact. David Geddis landed head first in a hedge, which softened his landing. Peter Canavan was less fortunate. He landed face downwards on the road and died almost instantaneously. It was a terrible tragedy, and it affected Geddis so badly that he asked to leave the club. He had frequently to drive past where the accident took place and it preyed on his mind.

Neither lad had been drinking. They were nice, decent young men returning home about 1.30 in the morning as they were perfectly entitled to do because it was after a match. Geddis owned the car and his mistake was to let his friend drive although Peter was a learner driver and they had no 'L' plates with them. By chance, the next car to drive along the empty road that night was a police car.

At 2 a.m. there was a knock at my door. 'Mr Robson, the manager of Ipswich Town?' said a policeman. 'Yes,' I said. 'I've got some sad news for you,' he said. 'Oh God,' I said. I thought he was going to tell me that one of my sons had died. 'There's been a fatal accident,' he said. 'One of your players is dead. Another one is injured.' It was almost like losing a member of the family. You work with these boys and get close to them. The cruel irony of it was that if they had been wearing seat belts Peter Canavan wouldn't have died.

David Geddis is an aggressive, fiery player with plenty of pace, but he hasn't quite made it, chiefly because he lacks the touch and technique. I sold him to Aston Villa for £300,000 and he has been mainly a reserve at Villa Park, as he had been at Ipswich.

Considering the amount of driving they do, few footballers and managers are involved in car crashes, but there have been many near misses. One accident which failed to make the headlines was when Kevin Beattie overturned his Opel car some years ago and, along with John Wark and two young reserve players, Dale Roberts and Glen Westley, escaped unharmed.

The car was a write-off, and only one wheel and the battery were salvaged. Beattie had it insured for third party risks only, and as no other vehicle was involved he lost £1,400. We were training at Shotley that day, and I drove past a few minutes after the accident happened. Charlie Woods, who was a mile or two ahead of me, stopped when he saw the upturned car with its wheels still spinning and was standing in the road flagging me down. The car was squashed into a grotesque shape, yet miraculously Beattie, Wark, Roberts and Westley were able to climb out of a side window. It hit a bank and turned over three times before landing upside down.

Ipswich have not had the best kind of luck with car accidents. In December 1981, reserve defender Kevin Steggles was in a collision on his way to the ground to join the first-team coach for a trip to Middlesbrough. Fortunately he was not seriously hurt but was detained in hospital overnight with minor injuries. We were short of several first-team players that weekend, and it was just another problem for me at a worrying time.

A few days after the 1978 Cup Final, both Hunter and Beattie had knee operations. When the surgeon opened Beattie's knee he saw three pieces of cartilage loose around the joint. 'It's a wonder you can walk, let alone play football,' he said. Meanwhile Hunter had foreign bodies removed from his knee. I realised then how close we had been to seeing either or both of them break down at Wembley.

Twelve

Thijssen and Muhren

I was paid a bonus of £5,000 by Ipswich for helping the club to win the FA Cup, and after tax I had less than £2,000 left. I decided to spend the whole amount on a holiday for Elsie and the boys in Monte Carlo. Our family life had suffered because of the demands of the job, and I felt I had to repay them in some small way. We booked into the Beach Plaza Hotel, and staying at the same hotel were Sir Matt and Lady Jean Busby.

This was the time when Tottenham Hotspur paid £750,000 for Osvaldo Ardiles and Ricardo Villa, first of the overseas stars to play in English football when the Football League relaxed their ban on the hiring of foreign players. Matt and I discussed this development over a number of drinks and a couple of dinners and we agreed that £750,000 was a lot of money but that the deal would be worth it if Ardiles and Villa were as good as they looked on television playing for Argentina in the 1978 World Cup. Sir Matt is a very nice, kindly man and I got to know him well in those nine days.

In football it is hard to get to know people. A manager rushes in and out of dressing-rooms and boardrooms and has brief conversations with opponents and rivals, but rarely does he have the opportunity of long, meaningful discussions. I was grateful during that holiday for being given the chance to talk to one of the country's greatest managers and most respected figures.

We agreed that the idea of signing foreign players was sound providing the players were of high quality and could supply the skill and expertise which was sometimes lacking in our game. We also agreed that transfer fees in England were reaching such astronomical heights that it made good business sense for clubs to shop on the Continent.

In the Ipswich pre-season matches that summer we played in Holland, and during our stay I heard that Arnold Muhren, a left-side midfield player with Twente Enschede, was unsettled and wanted a transfer. I had seen Muhren play in a number of matches we had played at Enschede and I knew his ability. With Arsenal interested in Brian Talbot, and Hunter and Beattie both injured, I needed some reinforcements and Muhren seemed ideal for my needs.

Muhren's contract had expired and Ajax wanted to buy him. Twente, who were short of money, asked £150,000 for him and Ajax, equally short of money, were only prepared to pay £100,000. By English standards that was a low price, and I was determined to get him, especially after Ipswich lost 5–0 to Nottingham Forest in the FA Charity Shield, the opening match of the 1978–9 season.

That match was memorable for a couple of typical Brian Clough remarks. The first was a shouted comment to Ken Burns when Forest were leading 5–0 near the end. 'Hey Burnsie,' said Clough. 'We want six!'

One of the goals was a spectacular volley from Martin O'Neill, who shortly afterwards upset Clough when he failed to get a tackle in. Clough was quickly on his feet. 'Hey, Jimmy' he shouted at Jimmy Gordon, the Forest trainer, 'get him off and next week teach him how to defend.' O'Neill was duly taken off. Jimmy Gordon used to take the first-team training at that time. Clough was rarely seen at the training ground, and nor was Peter Taylor. I thought it was amusing that the manager should be telling his trainer to teach a player how to defend.

After the 1978 Cup Final I thought my team was near its zenith and was capable of remaining at the top for four years at least if we had good luck with injuries. But within a year seven of those players had gone and I was rebuilding once more. Trevor Whymark was sold to Vancouver Whitecaps, Talbot went to Arsenal, Geddis to Aston Villa, Mick Lambert to Cambridge, Roger Osborne to Colchester and Clive Woods to Norwich. In addition Hunter and Beattie were virtually finished by injuries.

Younger players like Terry Butcher, Russell Osman, Steve McCall, Eric Gates and Alan Brazil were coming through from the youth policy, but I still needed a few new signings. I made my mind up that Muhren would be the first. I telephoned Ton van Dalen, the manager of Twente Enschede, and quickly agreed a fee of £150,000. He gave me permission to speak to Muhren the next day.

On the Monday morning, I hired a five-seater plane and flew to Amsterdam to conduct the transfer. Time was short because new players had to be registered by the following Thursday if they were to be eligible for the first round of the European Cup Winners' Cup. I saw Muhren and he was happy with the terms I put to him. But he insisted: 'I can't decide anything until I talk to my wife. I will ring you later.'

That night he called again and said: 'I'm sorry, I cannot join you. My wife doesn't want to leave Holland.' Most managers would have accepted that, but I was persistent. 'Can I see your wife and talk to her?' I asked. Arnold spoke English well, but his wife's English was not so good. He came back and said she was agreeable but he wasn't hopeful of reaching the conclusion I sought.

I hailed a taxi outside the Amsterdam Hilton and was taken to the Muhrens' house in Volendam, a thirty-minute drive from Amsterdam. At first Mrs Muhren was extremely reluctant to accept my offer to fly to Ipswich the next day and tour the area to test how she liked it, but finally she agreed.

When we flew to England the next day, I asked the pilot to show the Muhrens the beautiful Suffolk countryside, and we even circled the ground while a practice match was going on. The players knew it was the plane I had hired, and they waved. 'Doesn't look too bad, does it, Arnold?' I said.

I knew Arnold was keen because, like many Dutch players, he was disillusioned with the diminishing support in domestic football in Holland. Top Dutch players rarely play in front of more than twenty thousand spectators, but at Portman Road that would be a fortnightly event for him – and away from home the crowds would often be much bigger still.

When it was time for the Muhrens to return home, I thought I had achieved my objective. 'Can I ring you tomorrow with a decision?' asked Arnold. 'Certainly,' I replied. I was confident of good news when his call came the following morning – only to be let down. 'I'm very sorry, but I cannot come,' he said.

By this time the news was in the Dutch newspapers and I thought there would be a stampede of Dutch clubs after him, and perhaps clubs from other countries. However, Ajax refused to increase their offer, and no other club was interested. I kept ringing van Dalen for I still believed I had a chance of signing Arnold. To my great delight, I finally received a message saying that he had changed his mind. He was willing to come to England after all.

He signed too late for the European Cup Winners' Cup deadline and made his début at home against Liverpool. We lost 0–3, and Arnold never had a worthwhile kick. He must have wondered what he had committed himself to for the next two years! When we had the ball, which wasn't often, it was played over his head most of the time.

Talbot was becoming increasingly despondent and I knew it was inevitable that we would soon lose him. He came to me and said that he wanted to join Arsenal because they were a bigger club and he would be more successful there.

I said: 'You played in the Cup Final. Who won?' 'We did,' he said. 'Well then,' I said. 'That's your answer.' I persuaded him to sign a new contract, but in the ensuing months his game suffered because of his agitation to leave. He never said anything at the time, but later I was to learn that his marriage had ended and he wanted to leave the area.

Talbot is a very honest person, and when he came to see me again, he said: 'I thought all this wouldn't affect my game but it has.' I agreed to sell him and the deal, worth £450,000, went through early in January. Arsenal are one of the best clubs to conduct business with, because they pay up on time, or, in this case, ahead of time. They put down £250,000 and paid off the remaining £200,000 a year later. Talbot had cost us nothing.

Within a month I signed his replacement, Frans Thijssen from Twente Enschede for half that amount, £200,000, and I rated it one of my best transfer coups to have bought two World Cup stars in Muhren and Thijssen for a combined outlay of £350,000. As with Muhren, the Thijssen deal was complex. At first, van Dalen was unwilling to sell immediately. 'You can have him when his contract expires at the end of the season,' he said.

But I couldn't wait that long. Arnold Muhren told me that Thijssen would be ideal in English conditions and advised me to get him as soon as possible. I kept calling van Dalen, and each time he said it would be impossible to bring forward the date when Thijssen would be available. But that winter football was affected by some of the worst weather conditions for years and the Dutch League was cancelled for six weeks, putting pressure on clubs like Twente just to survive. In the end, Twente ran so short of money that they were having difficulty paying the players, and my £200,000 for Thijssen meant salvation for them. Within a month of Talbot's departure, I had signed Thijssen and the arrival of the two Dutchmen led to a significant change in the way Ipswich played.

Instead of being a long-ball side, with the emphasis on reaching the front players as quickly as possible, we now played more through the midfield. These two skilful players gave us a new dimension. They complemented each other beautifully. Muhren was the passer, the player with a great eye for a pass. Thijssen was the dribbler, the player who ran at opponents, committed them and beat them. They gave us width, which was important. I feel sometimes that English players are haunted by the touchline. They don't like being out there. They prefer the intimacy of the centre of the pitch. But Thijssen and Muhren had the desire to play wide, and it transformed our approach.

Both men are superb trainers and among the finest professionals I have worked with in thirty years. I cannot think of anyone I would rate higher as a professional than Arnold Muhren. I would do anything for him. Whatever you ask him to do in training, he will do. No one works harder, and when a match is over, he won't go out drinking. He goes to bed. English players can learn from the example of these two. They have both been a credit to themselves and their country.

When the rule allowing clubs to employ foreign players was brought in, I am sure the authorities meant it to apply to good players from abroad who would make up for deficiencies in our game. Ardiles, for example, was a type of midfield player who is not to be found in English football. The same could be said about Muhren and Thijssen. We don't have players of this calibre, so it was justifiable to import them.

But many of the fifty or sixty overseas players now playing in English football are artisans, no different in style or technique to many English players. Some clubs, therefore, have abused this rule by bringing in mediocre players. There are exceptions, of course, but in my view many Yugoslavs have been admitted when they offer the same package as an English player – a willingness to work, competitiveness and aggression, and a limited amount of skill.

Muhren and Thijssen were the best signings made by an English club, better value I think than Ardiles and Villa at Spurs, because they were half the price and have not missed many games, whereas Villa has often been injured.

Thijssen had two or three spells out when he developed hamstring trouble. He has short hamstrings which are inclined to go, but his absences were not enough to stop him being elected the Footballer of the Year by the football writers in 1980–1. When his contract expired at the end of that season I spent many anxious weeks trying to persuade him to stay with us a further two years.

Coming to England had revived his career and he became one of Europe's leading footballers. At twenty-nine he felt he owed it to himself and his family to seek the best possible contract, and I didn't blame him for that. There was much speculation that he was about to join a Continental club, and there was a problem when he claimed that I said when I first signed him that I would let him go at the end of his contract for £60,000. I said that to Arnold, but not Frans, but the new contract we signed stipulated that he would be a free agent at the end of it. He was holidaying in Holland when he told me at last that he was willing to re-sign. Once more I flew to Holland. I wanted to make absolutely sure he was our player! The flight to Holland cost £60, as against £1,200 to Buenos Aires – another reason why I think we may have had the better bargain.

The rule allows clubs to sign up two players from abroad, but the way the British transfer market has escalated – it is now the priciest in the world and almost totally divorced from financial reality – there is now a case for an open house. If it is possible to buy a good player for £100,000 from abroad, why pay a million pounds in England? It is good business to buy the right kind of players from other countries.

It has been said that English cricket is failing to produce enough good young players because too many jobs are held by West Indians, Pakistanis, Indians and Australians, and that could be applied to football as well. But I say to English players that they should take a hard look at themselves and ask themselves whether they are working hard enough. Are they showing enough professionalism and dedication? It is in their hands. The challenge of competing against foreign players should improve their game. I am sure playing behind Arnold Muhren has made Steve McCall a better player at Ipswich.

It was said when the foreign players were first admitted that they wouldn't stand up to the forty-two match slog of the English season, through rain, snow and ice, but that has been proved a myth. Ardiles has shown he stands up to these conditions better than most English professionals. The experiment has been a success, but I wish more English players were able to match the professionalism of Muhren, Thijssen and Ardiles.

Thirteen

Time on the Grass

We have a phrase at Ipswich Town Football Club which explains why we produce more of our own players than almost any other club in the Football League. It is 'Time on the grass.'

When we sign an apprentice, we work him hard on the practice pitches or in the gym. We teach him how to play football and he has a better chance of making the grade in our soccer academy than the equivalent young player at the bigger clubs.

These boys are the club's lifeblood. They're important people and we treat them as such. Ipswich cannot afford to compete with the big money clubs who chase after the England Schoolboy stars, so we work in areas which are neglected by the richer clubs, like the North of Scotland and Cumberland.

The Ipswich team that played in the Final of the UEFA Cup cost £600,000 in transfer fees and seven of the players – Mick Mills, Steve McCall, Russell Osman, Terry Butcher, John Wark, Alan Brazil and Eric Gates – cost nothing.

These days, £600,000 doesn't buy an average First Division player. So if Ipswich can do it, why don't more clubs invest their money in producing their own players instead of buying someone else's? The answer is that the average manager doesn't survive in his job long enough to implement a successful youth policy.

It takes a minimum of three years to groom a young player, often longer, but now many managers in the First Division last three years in their post? The directors make bad appointments, the manager and his staff go, and another managerial team moves in with different ideas. More often than not, the young players are released. The wastage is enormous.

At Portman Road we work harder at it than they do at other clubs and I think our staff are better judges of whether a young player is going to make the grade. We have just one full-time scout, John

Carruthers, who operates in the North, and seven part-time scouts and we estimate it costs us £80,000 a year to maintain our scouting system. We spend a further £20,000 a year on running expenses, so for a total of £100,000 we are able to produce enough good players to keep Ipswich near the top of the pile.

Each season we sign on four or five apprentices after staging a series of trials in different parts of the country. We pay these youngsters twenty-five pounds a week and provide a further fifteen pounds a week for their board and lodging. Roughly half fail to make the grade, and I feel that is one of the saddest parts of my job – having to tell a young man that he will never become a star.

We would produce better players in this country if League clubs were allowed to sign youngsters on earlier and give them expert coaching at a vital stage of their careers. But League regulations forbid clubs from signing apprentices until their seventeenth birthdays, and schoolboys are not allowed to train at a club until they are thirteen.

On the Continent boys can train at clubs from the age of eight, and this could be one of the reasons why continental players have more skill than the average English player. In the formative years youngsters learn good habits. Here, our youngsters are playing competitive matches in schools, urged on by parents and teachers who are more interested in winning than the acquisition of the basic skills.

George Burley, whom I consider to be the best attacking right-back in the British Isles, is a good example of how Ipswich recruit their players. George was recommended by George Findlay, our Scottish scout, and we arranged for him to take part in a private trial at Troon, in Ayrshire, along with a number of other players we were interested in.

Ipswich paid for the ground, the gear, the referee and linesmen – everything in fact – but when I arrived, there were five hundred people inside the ground including Bob Shankly, then manager of Hibernian.

I said to George Findlay: 'How did they get in? I thought it was supposed to be private.' George said it was impossible to stop them getting in.

George Burley was a small, frail fifteen-year-old and played at left-back in those days. I could see he had the attributes to become a good player, and we signed him on, despite the attentions of Bob Shankly and the other scouts who were present.

One of the boys among the thirty-two taking part that day was a lad named Kelly, whom John Carruthers said was one of the best prospects he had ever seen. 'The trouble is,' said John, 'he's Manchester United daft.'

So as not to attract too much attention, I asked that young Kelly shouldn't come on until the second half. He played for just twelve minutes and I stepped on to the pitch and said: 'You come off, son.' He looked disappointed, but I had seen enough. He was a very skilled player – a certainty, I thought, to become an international class player. We were unable to persuade him to sign, however, and he went to Old Trafford. I never heard of him again. He didn't make it, and we signed George Burley instead. George got into our first team at seventeen, and except for injury has been there ever since.

In another trial at Shotley in 1972 we signed Eric Gates, brother of former Middlesbrough centre-half Bill Gates, together with John Peddelty, Tommy Parkin, Robin Turner, John Stirk and Mike Brolly, who later went to Chelsea. That was one of the vintage years, because we won the F A Youth Cup the following season. Eric Gates was a midfield player at the time and we weren't sure which was his best position. He was sharp over short distances and had good control, but couldn't do the mileage for a midfield player. After three years, we finally decided he was better as a front player and, having cleared up a few problems, he finally established himself in the first team.

One of my best signings was Kevin Beattie. I was on a trip to Zambia in 1971, billeted out with Cyril Lea at the home of a businessman named Don Lightfoot, when I first heard Beattie's name mentioned. Beattie had gone to Liverpool for a trial and when he found that no one was at the station to meet him he went home again. Bill Shankly apparently said that if Beattie hadn't the initiative to find his own way to Anfield he didn't want him.

Don Lightfoot put me on to a friend of his, John Carruthers, who was to become my only full-time scout, and John said he had seen Beattie and agreed that he was a good prospect although his background was against him. John went to see Kevin at his home in Carlisle and gave him a ticket to go to Ipswich for a trial. Ron Gray, our chief scout, met Beattie at the station and discovered that he had only sixpence on him and a pair of boots that looked as though they had been rejected by Oxfam.

Kevin may have looked scruffy, but once we fitted him out in

Top: With Mick Mills, the captain who has been with me from the start of my career at Ipswich. In an era when football generally has been short of outstanding captains, Mick has been one of the finest leaders since the war.

Above: An anxious moment on the bench at one of our European games. On my left is Eric Gates. On my right is Cyril Lea, and next to him John Wark.

Below: With Bobby Roberts, the Colchester manager, and Keith Fletcher, captain of Essex and England, after a benefit match at Colchester. In the summer, when I have the time, I often go along to Essex matches.

At the Coliseum, Rome, before the infamous U E F A Cup tie against Lazio in 1973. Standing on the wall with me are Cyril Lea and Dr Brian Simpson, the club's former medical officer. On my left are Ken Brightwell, a director, David Johnson, Clive Woods, Allan Hunter and Kevin Beattie. We didn't know it at the time, but the following night we were to be cast in the role of Christians thrown to the lions in the Olympic Stadium.

Eric Gates is probably on the receiving end of more violent tackles than any other player in the English game. Here is a typical example. The defender has gone in from the side, nowhere near the ball, and caught Eric on the knee with his studs. After a match Eric's legs are often black and blue, but he will insist on playing in the next one.

Arnold Muhren and Frans Thijssen, the Dutchmen from Twente Enschede, whom I rate among my finest signings. Arnold arrived in August 1978 for £150,000, and is probably the finest professional I have ever been associated with. Frans came the following February, having cost £220,000, and in the 1980–81 season was voted 'Footballer of the Year' by the Football Writers' Association.

The moment a manager treasures. We have beaten my old club WBA in the semi-final of the FA Cup at Highbury in 1978, and we are going on to Wembley. Here I am enjoying a joke with John Cobbold. That was the year we went on and won the Cup.

On the pitch at Wembley after winning the 1978 F A Cup. A photographer tries to arrange us in a group, but the best pictures on these occasions are usually the impromptu ones.

Opposite: I try to say a few words to the vast crowd outside the Ipswich Town Hall the day after Ipswich won the F A Cup. With me are two of the players who helped make it possible: Kevin Beattie, whose career was sadly ended by injuries to his right knee, and Allan Hunter, who played at Wembley when not fully fit and needed an operation shortly afterwards.

Some of the people who have helped make Ipswich a successful football club through our 'time on the grass' policy. With me, left to right, are Cyril Lea, who left to join Stoke, and then Hull; Charlie Woods, who is in charge of the reserves; Bobby Ferguson, the first-team coach; and Ron Gray, the chief scout. Beside the familiar F A Cup is the Football Combination Cup.

The agony of waiting . . .

. . . and the joy and elation that success can bring! Terry Butcher's sixty-fourth-minute goal in the Mungersdorfer Stadium in Cologne had just given us a 2–0 lead in the second leg of the U E F A Cup semi-final on 22 April 1981. We were through to the final.

Arriving back at Southend Airport with the UEFA Cup. British Air Ferries even went to the trouble of putting the Ipswich crest on the door.

The 1981 squad which won the UEFA Cup. Back row (*left to right*): Bobby Robson, John Wark, Russell Osman, Paul Cooper, Terry Butcher, Arnold Muhren, Steve McCall, Bobby Ferguson. Front row: Frans Thijssen, Eric Gates, Mick Mills, Paul Mariner, Alan Brazil.

With Patrick Cobbold, the Ipswich chairman, and England manager Ron Greenwood at the home game against Swansea City on 7 November 1981. If I am looking rather tight-lipped, it is because Ipswich lost 3–2.

Playing in a charity match with managerial colleagues Ron Atkinson, who seems to be sharing my anxiety, and John Bond. Managers love to play the game when they have a chance . . . even if their bodies won't let them!

a new pair of boots and some gear he looked like a king. He excited me as soon as I saw him kick the ball, and it was no surprise when he was picked for the England Under-23 side at the age of eighteen.

By the time he was twenty he was in the full England side at left-back. He was another Duncan Edwards, a power player who had every asset to become one of the all-time greats. Unfortunately, luck went against him and he suffered the cruellest of knee injuries. His troubles started in October 1977 when he came on as substitute for Dave Watson in the final twenty minutes of a World Cup game in Luxembourg.

When he arrived home, he said his knee was troubling him and we pulled him out of the next match. A specialist advised a cartilage operation, but when he started playing again after the injury, Kevin said the knee still wasn't right. He had another operation to remove the other cartilage, then an operation to repair the ligaments and a fourth to tidy up some floating bodies. Altogether he had five operations on his right knee, the leg he jumped off, and, not surprisingly, it affected his performance. He was one of the outstanding headers of a ball in the game, but after so much surgery the spring had gone from his jump and he was unable to climb quite as he had done earlier in his career. He now has an arthritic knee. It is a tragedy ... for him and for England.

Steve McCall, one of the First Division's most improved players, also comes from Carlisle but made a less sensational impact than Kevin when he first arrived at Portman Road after being recommended by John Carruthers. I thought he was a borderline case after seeing him play in a trial. He might make it or he might not. John persuaded me to take him. 'He can do better than that,' he said. I took a gamble and signed him. He was a late developer, and I am glad I took the risk because he quickly became one of the club's most consistent and adaptable players.

Russell Osman was recommended by my brother Tom who had seen him playing for Derby Schools. The son of Rex Osman, a former professional with Derby County, Russell had played schoolboy rugby for England and had a rather physical approach to the game. He was a good tackler but too ready to whack opponents and we had to curb his enthusiasm in his early days.

Aston Villa and Derby were also chasing him, but we signed him after watching him play in a trial match against Norwich City. He impressed me straight away. He was tough, two-footed and had a good attitude for a defender. In many ways, he reminded me of Kevin Beattie.

Playing in the same trial match was a young man I later discovered was Kevin Bond, son of John Bond. I didn't know who he was at the time and asked Ken Brown, then the assistant manager of Norwich.

Ken looked around him and said: 'He's the boss's son.' I replied: 'He can't play.' Ken made a non-committal shrug, but we were both to be proved wrong. Kevin Bond persevered against the odds and finally emerged as a First Division player in his own right.

Terry Butcher, the other half of our central defensive partnership, like Russell Osman cost us nothing. Terry was a quiet, sensitive lad who played for Lowestoft Schools and trained with us. He was an elegant, sophisticated player with a good delivery and a sound tackle, but he lacked confidence. He has since overcome that problem and has deserved his promotion to the senior England side.

Alan Brazil is a player who was made by the Ipswich system. When he joined us, recommended by George Findlay, he had a great left foot and little else, but I sensed he had the qualities to become a top-class striker. We worked on him, developing his control and his positional play, and he was soon replacing Trevor Whymark, one of our successes in the seventies.

After Ipswich won the FA Cup for the first time in 1978, I looked at the team and said to myself: 'That team will serve us for the next five years.' But within three years half of the players had gone: Roger Osborne, Allan Hunter, Brian Talbot, David Geddis, Clive Woods and the substitute Mick Lambert.

It is a credit to the club's scouts and training staff that we were able to provide first-class replacements of international ability – players like Osman, Butcher, Brazil and McCall. Cyril Lea, Bobby Ferguson, Charlie Woods, Brian Owen and our scouts – Ron Gray, the chief scout, John Carruthers, chief North-East scout, and George Findlay, the Scottish scout – have worked selflessly and loyally over the years, and the credit for our success is largely due to them. They know, like me, what 'Time on the grass' means.

Fourteen

Geeing Them Up

The thirty minutes before a game and the ten minutes at half-time are the times when a manager earns his money. Payday for the manager is the day of the match. The rest of what he does is incidental to that. The phrase which is commonly used to cover his activities in this time is motivation. It is a word I rarely use myself. I believe the manager has a dual role in these vitally important minutes. He has to tell his players how he wants them to play, explain the tactical side, and he has to get them in the right mood. He must make sure their attitude is right for the task ahead.

I believe we are superior to most European countries when it comes to attitude. An example of what I mean came in the UEFA Cup fourth round away leg against St Etienne on 4 March 1981. We won that match in the tunnel before the players went out!

It was a crucial match for Ipswich Town Football Club. St Etienne were the favourites to win the competition, the outstanding club side in France, and few foreign sides went there and won. We arrived three hours before the kick-off and the ground was already packed with forty-two thousand people waving green flags and banners. It was a knife-edge atmosphere and it made my players more keyed up than they would have been normally.

I stressed to them the importance of putting on a good performance, because the whole of Europe was looking at us. Psychologically, the players were in the best possible frame of mind when the time came to line up with the St Etienne players in the tunnel before the officials led us out on to the pitch.

As the two teams stood shoulder to shoulder, the Ipswich players were almost snarling like guard dogs. 'Errrrrrrr,' they grunted. 'Come on, let's get at them. Errrrrrrrrr. Let's get among 'em.' Six-footers like Terry Butcher, Russell Osman and Paul Mariner were towering over their frightened-looking opponents. At the back of the line, Bobby Ferguson and I couldn't stop laughing. Our performance that night was one of the best I have seen from an English club in Europe.

It was one of the few times in my managerial career where I came in and said only a few words of congratulations. Usually just saying 'well done' isn't enough when the team has played well. I generally go into the reasons why the team played well, so that next time they will do the same thing. I will go over points and make sure the players realised why the game went their way.

When they first joined us, Arnold Muhren and Frans Thijssen were surprised at the way we gee players up. In Holland it doesn't happen, nor, I believe, does it happen in many countries. It may explain why our players appear to be more committed than foreign players. English players want to win more, and that is a commendable approach.

Of course it can work the other way, and there may be times when the manager has to calm a player down when he has become over-excited. One such time was before an England 'B' match in Prague in 1980, when I was manager. The player was Mick Lyons, who was then with Everton. He stormed round the dressing-room shouting 'Aggression, aggression' at the top of his voice and banging his head into his hand. The pitch was frozen, and I thought that if he went out there in that mood he wouldn't last very long. He would be the first person to be sent off.

I usually go into the dressing-room at 2.30 for the final talk with the players, having already had a team talk the day before. Muhren and Thijssen are quiet, unemotional people who need little in the way of stimulation, but Butcher, Osman, Steve McCall and Kevin O'Callaghan are among the players who need a bit of a gee up. Alan Brazil used to but is improving now that he has developed into one of the leading strikers in the Football League. For all his experience, Paul Mariner still needs a little talk before he goes on to the field.

Mick Mills is very sensible and listens to ideas. So, too, does George Burley. Both men also contribute ideas. I never discourage players from putting their own point of view in any situation. However silly the idea, I never say: 'That's a load of rubbish.' If I disagree with it, I will try to talk them round to my way of thinking.

Players look for discipline and advice before and after games. They will see it as a sign of weakness if the manager just lets them get on with it. They all need help, even the most experienced pros, and often reassurance. Football is a very psychological game and if it starts going against your players, anxieties creep in and confidence starts to ebb away. Once the tide starts running out, it can be hard to reverse it.

The role of the manager has become more important in recent years, so much so that some people say it has become *too* important. The Press are usually more interested in what the manager says than what the players say. Ron Greenwood is one of those who insist that it is primarily a players' game, not a managers' game. He is right, of course, but it cannot be denied that managers now play a more prominent part than at any time in the game's history.

The pressure is on them to win matches, so they have to be personalities in their own right who can handle that pressure. If the team fails, it's the manager's failure, not the team's failure. So, if the manager is the one who pays the price of defeat, then he should be the key figure. Many of the leading managers are good talkers, men like Malcolm Allison, Tommy Docherty, Brian Clough, Ron Atkinson, Alan Mullery, John Bond and Lawrie McMenemy. Talking – to players, the Press and the public – is a key part of the job. One of our most respected managers, Dave Sexton, lost his job at Old Trafford partly because he was a quiet type who didn't project the image wanted by the Manchester United directors.

But the public will only accept the talkative, controversial managers if they win more matches than they lose, if they are successful. Despite the elevation of the football manager to the equivalent of a showbiz personality, there is still room for the quiet type to succeed. Bob Paisley, for example, remains a quiet, homespun person who would be far happier sitting at home in his carpet slippers watching racing on television than being interviewed by Jimmy Hill on *Match of the Day*. Tony Waddington was a steady, sober type who did a good job over the years and so too, of course, does Dave Sexton. Jim Smith at Oxford and John Barnwell when he was at Wolverhampton are two more of the same type. There is no identikit of the football manager. It takes all kinds of personalities to do the job.

One of the necessary qualities is to be able to go into a dressing-room and berate players in a manner which wouldn't be tolerated in any other industry. If a shop floor manager spoke to his men the way I sometimes speak to my players, the whole factory would walk out on strike!

I estimate that I have to rant and rave in one match in three ... and I have one of the best sides in the country. There have been times when I have had rows with players, but I know and they know that these have been necessary. A good player will respond to criticism. If the manager is slap happy and indifferent, the players will become slap happy and indifferent. If you are unprofessional, you get nothing.

A time when I was very angry was during the UEFA Cup Final second leg against AZ 67 Alkmaar in the Olympic Stadium, Amsterdam on 20 May 1981. We led 3–0 after the first leg at Portman Road, and although Frans Thijssen scored early on, we allowed the Dutchmen to over-run us, particularly in midfield. With nothing to lose, AZ coach Georg Kessler had his team playing what I call 'total risk football.' They had only two players at the back marking Paul Mariner and Alan Brazil, and often they were playing 5–3–2, with sweeper Johnny Metgod, a fine player, playing in midfield and attack.

AZ flooded the midfield and put in a string of crosses which Butcher and Osman, so dominant in the air throughout the season, often failed to clear. Our midfield players weren't tracking their midfield players, the marking was poor, and in some cases players weren't working hard enough.

The trainers' seats were a long way from the pitch and I had been unable to make myself heard. I shouted so much that I was almost hoarse by the end. At half-time, I tore into the players.

We were still in a sound position, 5–3 up on aggregate, but if we continued playing like that we could still lose. Part of the trouble was that Eric Gates, whose strongest points do not include marking and picking up opponents, was being lost by Metgod, so I told John Wark to take over that job, releasing Gates for the Dane Nygaard, who played a much less influential role.

We tightened up in the second half and only conceded one more goal, winning 5–4 over the two legs. The only goal of the half, a stunning free kick taken by Jonkers, was an example of how good planning can save goals. Ipswich have an agreed number of players who are deputed to go into the wall at any free kick – five if it is in a dangerous position in front of goal, four if it is on an angle further out, and three if it is some way out. Goalkeeper Paul Cooper wanted four men, but there were only three when Jonkers struck his shot. We had an inquest later about that one!

I have an instant replay type of memory for incidents. I am able to recall almost every move during a game and talk about it several days later. I never bother to take notes. It is all in my mind. I can be watching football on television at home and say to Elsie: 'Watch this, they're going to score soon.' Alf Ramsey was a master at recalling incidents and build-up play. Many managers are: it's a trick of the trade. A few managers take notes. Bill Nicholson used to, but he also had a sound memory.

I was exhausted at the end of the AZ 67 match. It took more out of me than almost any previous match when I had been in charge. It meant so much to me. If Ipswich had failed to win the UEFA Cup after being in a position to win the Treble at one stage, I think I might have quit the club. I had a feeling that maybe I had gone as far as I could at Portman Road, and that perhaps it was time for a new challenge. I was sure I could do a similar job at another club – building up a squad of young players without making million-pound buys and turning them into a side worthy of winning the League championship.

As we were about to leave Southend Airport for the trip to Amsterdam on the Monday, a journalist told me that Lawrie McMenemy had turned down the opportunity to become manager of Manchester United. I said I was surprised at the news. Like most people in football, I assumed Lawrie would be taking the job. However, I have turned down numerous jobs in the past myself, and I understood his reasons.

In the newspapers the next day I found myself being connected with the Manchester United job. I was already in a position where I could have had the Sunderland manager's position. It was unwanted pressure. The headlines should have been about the AZ game, not my personal position.

After the first leg at Portman Road, a similar question had been put to me. 'Would I stay at Ipswich if we failed to win?' I cast some doubt on it. After the second leg, Mick Mills was quoted as saying it had been unfair that I had put pressure on the players by intimating that if they didn't win, I would leave.

Mick was right. I had put pressure on the players. A manager has to do that. It was another way of helping to make sure that Ipswich didn't throw away a 3–0 lead. Football is a game of pressure, but managers experience much, much more of it than the players. If a team loses, the players are unlikely to be sacked. But the manager's job is on the line very time his team takes the field.

After the Amsterdam game I would have liked to stay in the dressing-room to experience with the players the delight of winning a major trophy. We had ridden the precipice for much of that game, and I would have liked to have wound down a little with the players and enjoy it with them. It was a time when a manager feels a certain closeness with the players. However, the TV and Press men wanted me and I had to leave.

The manager has to judge the right time and place to be critical, especially when his team has played badly in the opening forty-five minutes. To go storming into the dressing-room abusing them can be counter-productive and lower their confidence still further. As you get older, so you get wiser and you can judge the time for chastisement and the time for discretion. I feel that I am able to get on with players of all ages. There need not be a generation gap in football.

Before our overseas matches and nearly all our home games, we have a warm-up, either on the pitch or, if we are at Portman Road, in the gym, which has a large Astroturf playing surface. I believe warm-ups are essential and our football would be better if the idea was more generally tried out, especially at international level. Unfortunately it is not always possible for a League side to go out for a warm-up when playing at another club's ground. In the middle of winter, some clubs do not like the opposition tearing up the pitch.

During the 1979–80 season I had a letter from two psychologists at Birmingham University, Dr John Gardner and Dr Will Davies, who were interested in visiting Ipswich and finding out why we were so successful in competition against the big city clubs. I had an open mind about the idea. I know the Brazilians employ psychologists, but the idea has not been properly tried in this country.

I had previously doubted whether non-footballing people could be of any assistance. The football manager is a kind of psychologist himself, if only an amateur at it. But I wrote back and invited them to spend a few weeks with us. They said they were particularly interested in the psychology of a team playing at Anfield. They wanted to know why teams never won at Liverpool and whether there were any other reasons other than football ones for this remarkable record.

As we were soon to be playing at Anfield, I thought they could help us. They asked me why I thought Liverpool never lost at home. I said: 'First because they're the best team and second because of the crowd and the atmosphere.'

They spoke to the players who said the same as I had said. After a series of interviews which I think the players enjoyed, the two doctors recommended that we should arrive at Anfield early and go out on the pitch, firstly to sample the atmosphere and secondly to stage a twenty-minute warm-up. 'Let them get used to everything, so it's not new to them,' they said. We took their advice – and drew 1–1. I do not say that their advice was the main factor in halting our bad run at Anfield. The football we played that day was the primary factor. But it may have made a slight difference . . . and that could be the missing ingredient.

Another suggestion they made was that we should install a clock in the home dressing-room at Portman Road. They said they noticed that players were always asking the time in the thirty minutes before kick-off – a sign of their anxiety. A clock would help relieve that. We now have a clock, but some of the players now say: 'Is that clock right?'

They asked the players what they disliked most about their job and the players were unanimous: they hated travelling. Most of our travelling is done by coach, and some players play cards and others read but they still find it boring. They complained that the television set wasn't working properly.

The psychologists recommended that we install video which did work and we now have two television sets. We find long journeys pass more easily. They also listened to my team talks and said they thought I was a good lecturer. I can talk for a long time without notes and they considered I had a future in university life! However, they thought I could spell out points more specifically to certain players and I have taken that advice. Sometimes I repeat things and say: 'Now are you sure you have understood that?' In the excitement of big matches, players can listen and not absorb what the manager says. Since the Birmingham experts were with us, I feel I have put that right.

I believe there is a place for the part-time psychological helper in football. He can point out obvious things which the harassed manager may have missed. But the manager has to be careful he doesn't find himself being usurped. A good manager is a psychologist, a father figure, a friend and a motivator. He has to do all those tasks himself. They are part of his job.

Fifteen

Where are the Coaches?

I despair sometimes when I think about the future of coaching in this country. Where are the experienced players, nearing the end of their careers, who have the ability to become the Bill Nicholsons and Ron Greenwoods of the nineties? I don't see many. In fact, I cannot see anyone in this category. I worry about the game. I am concerned about who is going to pass knowledge on to the next generation.

People who say footballers don't need coaching are idiots. Whatever job we do, we can all profit from the experiences and knowledge of other people. More so in football because it is a team game with eleven performers reliant on each other. The more those players understand each other, the better the team will play. Ipswich didn't become the best footballing side in Britain in the 1980–1 season by just going out and playing.

It was done on the training ground and in the gym. It was worked at over a period of years. We worked at individual skills as well as team skills. We evolved a style of playing that was suited to the players we had – Eric Gates playing just behind two central strikers Paul Mariner and Alan Brazil, and Frans Thijssen and Arnold Muhren playing wide in midfield.

Every player, no matter how much natural talent he has, can be helped by good coaching. That even applied to George Best, who had it all. George usually did everything right, but maybe he could have been advised about when to release the ball. There were times in matches when he might have helped his side more if he had passed instead of holding on to the ball.

In 1958 I remember Walter Winterbottom, the pioneer of coaching in this country, saying to a group of players that included Don Howe and myself: 'Look, you can become coaches. You should take a deeper interest in the game and pass on your knowledge.'

It had a profound effect on me. At Fulham Ron Greenwood and Jimmy Hill were already disciples of Winterbottom. Don Howe and I soon joined them. I went on FA courses and undertook lowly paid coaching jobs. I used to drive sixty miles to Oxford to coach the Oxford University side. Sixty miles there and sixty miles back, and I wasn't paid a mileage rate. I was paid two guineas a time and the three sessions I did a week added a third to my weekly income.

I did it because I wanted to further my career and because I needed the money. I don't see players doing things like that today. There is no incentive for them to do it. The top players earn up to £50,000 a year and they don't need the money.

They are taking a lot out of the game but not putting much back. Some of them believe that when they stop playing they can apply for a manager's job and become an instant manager without doing the necessary preparation.

I will tell them this: unless they have experience of speaking in front of footballers and putting their coaching ideas across, they have no chance of making it. Within a year or two they are a statistic on the managerial scrapheap. This is one of the major reasons why so many managers are sacked in the Football League. Too many men are appointed who do not have the right qualifications.

There are too many bad appointments by directors who have little knowledge about the abilities of the men they appoint. They see a name and think that he should make a successful manager. It is done in many cases by trial and error. It is a shameful way of conducting one of our major industries. In manufacturing, for instance, the directors don't pull a man off the shop floor and appoint him factory manager. Executives need training and qualifications. But in football the idea persists that a footballer, unused to coaching players or handling the business side of the game, can suddenly learn these responsibilities in a matter of days once he is put in the managerial chair.

I look at my playing staff at Ipswich and wonder who could become a manager. The name of Mick Mills springs to mind because he is my senior player. Possibly he could make it. But I would like to see him doing more about it. I would like to see more experienced players planning for their future by taking coaching courses and working at that side of the game.

Running a football club is a big responsibility. You are in charge of a footballing factory, and are answerable to up to forty thousand or more people in your area. A manager is constantly making decisions. He needs to know the game and the people in it.

To succeed, you need more than a big name and a host of international caps. What happened to the England players who won the World Cup in 1966 is a case in point. Although eight went in to management, only one of them has enjoyed any success as a manager. The solitary exception is Jack Charlton. He is a good coach and had a sound coaching background before he became manager of Middlesbrough and, later, Sheffield Wednesday.

Gordon Banks, Bobby Moore, Nobby Stiles, Alan Ball, Martin Peters, Bobby Charlton and Geoff Hurst have all managed clubs, and none has been a conspicuous success.

The arrival of the £1,000-a-week footballer has meant that today's players are able to save enough money through their pensions, which are payable when they retire, to set up in business. Some become very successful in business, like the former England forward Francis Lee. But many, lacking a proper business training, rely on other people and lose their money.

In West Germany and Italy, the two leading European nations in World Cup football in post-war years, it is much harder to obtain coaching and managerial qualifications than it is in England. In West Germany, no coach can get a job with a Bundesliga club until he has passed the five stages of certification, a process that lasts four years. The German clubs encourage their players to attend courses at a centre near Cologne, and you will often see top players attending the courses from Monday to Friday before reporting back to their clubs for a weekend match. That is how important the German clubs consider coaching and learning.

The West German coaching diploma is a twenty-four-week course. I think that a similar system should be employed in the Football League. If every manager had first to pass through this equivalent of a university course, I feel that fewer of them would fail. Of course a man's personality must come into it. It is useless having all the qualifications if he can't handle players and talk to them. To undergo such rigorous tests, however, it is practically impossible to survive without the right kind of personality.

Allen Wade, the FA Director of Coaching, launched a new advanced course in 1982 which requires four hundred hours of study. At the end of it, the student can earn a diploma similar to the one in West Germany. I feel that is a step in the right direction, but first the directors of football clubs must recognise these awards. At various gatherings of chairmen in the past two years, there has been support expressed for the view that managers should be better qualified and that clubs ought not to appoint men who have no coaching qualifications. Unfortunately this is never carried through. Too many under-prepared managers are still being appointed.

According to Allen Wade, significantly fewer older players of top quality are taking FA courses now than there were when he first started his job in 1960. He agrees that this is bad for our game and something needs to be done about it.

The Professional Footballers' Association and the Football League do all they can to encourage players to learn more about the game, but they can't force people to do it. Players taking courses have grants available from the Vocational Trust, so it is not a question of not being able to afford it.

Roughly seventy players every year sit the FA Full Badge, which until the arrival of the diploma was the highest award in our coaching scheme. About twenty-five per cent pass each year, which, considering that football is our biggest sport with roughly a million players, is not a very high percentage.

There is a commonly held idea that some players are reluctant to take courses because they will be brainwashed and programmed towards certain ideas. There is still a deeply held suspicion inside the game of the coaching scheme which owes its existence to Walter Winterbottom.

In my view such fears are groundless. I go to Lilleshall most years for the summer course, and it is more an exchange of ideas than a programming by FA coaches. Some of the world's leading coaches attend. It is like going back to university to freshen up your ideas and thoughts about football.

At many League clubs the training consists mainly of running, because the people in charge of it don't have a football brain. They have lazy minds and few training ideas. When you go to Lilleshall, you have a variety of ideas put before you which you can either accept and develop yourself, or reject.

Training should be about devising interesting ways of developing individual and team skills. Most football training grounds are empty in the afternoon because the coaches can't think of anything to fill the time available. They excuse the players because they know that if they gave them too much of their limited repertoire of ideas, the players would soon be bored. This lack of coaching expertise is reflected on the field on Saturday afternoons.

Of course it is very easy to over-work players in training, so that they are no longer fresh by the time the match comes round. Playing two matches a week is another factor which interrupts coaching programmes. A two-hour session is usually long enough even for the fittest players. But there are other ways of filling in the time, ways that can be made interesting for the players. Good players and good technique are fashioned on the training pitch, and just as a golfer needs to practice for hours to improve his swing, so do footballers need to practise.

A good coach is a mixture of the people who have influenced him. I suppose there is a lot of Winterbottom and Greenwood in me, but also much of Vic Buckingham and Bill Dodgin. There is also something of Dick Graham. Good coaching consists of integrating ideas from every possible source and making the best use of them. It is about making players and teams better. It is about making players think. We play so much football in this country that we probably spend less time learning the game and improving our skills than they do in many comparable countries. This is why I think it is vital to reduce the size of the First Division from twenty-two to eighteen clubs.

I also think the England manager should be more involved in the coaching scene, with closer contact between his department and the coaching department. Alf Ramsey wasn't coach orientated and his successor Don Revie didn't work with the coaching section either. Ron Greenwood did, but there could be a much closer relationship.

Sixteen

The Treble

In the 1980–1 season Ipswich failed in their bid to become the first club to do the Treble – win the First Division championship, the FA Cup and the UEFA Cup – but I remain convinced that this feat can be done. The club that does it will need more luck with injuries than we had, however. If George Burley, who missed nearly half the season, Kevin Beattie, who was able to play only intermittently, Paul Cooper, Mick Mills, Frans Thijssen, Paul Mariner and Eric Gates had played more often than they did, particularly in key matches, we might have succeeded.

You need high-class players, and I believe we had high-class players. But no manager can legislate against injury when those players are playing two or more competitive matches a week towards the end of the season. It was said that we might have scraped through if we had players of better quality in reserve. Perhaps that is true, but good players these days are not content to be reserves for months on end. There is a limit to the size of a first-team squad. I know that when I was a player I would not have tolerated playing for months in the Football Combination with no other incentive to sustain me than the knowledge that maybe the player in my position in the first team might go down injured.

A club winning the Treble needs to play a minimum of fifty-seven matches in a season, forty-two in the Football League, nine in the European or European Cup Winners Cup, six in the FA Cup. If it is in the UEFA Cup the total becomes sixty, because the UEFA Cup has an extra round and a two-leg final. In the 1980–1 season, Ipswich played a total of sixty-six matches. The previous season Arsenal played sixty-nine, because they had so many replays.

The Continentals laugh at us when they are told these statistics.

The Cologne officials whom we met in the UEFA Cup said: 'You English are crazy. It is impossible to play as many matches as that.'

Playing so many games leaves too little time for coaches to work on the skills of the players. I believe this is a primary reason why our players, or some of them, may be inferior to the best Continental players in technique. We lead in attitude and commitment, but lag behind in skill.

The size of the Football League must soon be reduced, with the smaller clubs going part-time. It amazes me that so many clubs can continue in business. The League should be based on quality, not quantity, with the uneconomic stragglers left to fall out when they are no longer strong enough to come up to the starting-line.

An eighteen-strong First Division must come soon, and when it does it will mean that the Treble-chasing clubs are committed to a minimum of fifty-nine matches, which is more realistic although still too high by European standards. If there are fewer matches, the clubs will need more income to cover their costs and this can come from a variety of sources, including the pools companies, who I believe get the copyright of the League fixtures far too cheaply, and the sponsorship of major competitions.

When the 1980–1 season started I believed Ipswich could be contenders to challenge Liverpool for the title because of our form in the second half of the previous season, when we climbed from near the bottom to finish third. Most managers start off by saying they are confident of doing well, but few believe it. I believed it, however, and so did the players.

In a season which stretches over ten months, there are peaks and lows for the manager, times of great joy and also times of depression. The manager has to try and maintain stability. When the team does well, he must make sure the players are not carried away by success and become lax. When they lose, he must restore their confidence. He has to use every situation he can to the advantage of his team, providing he keeps within the rules.

To outline what is involved, I did a match-by-match analysis of the Ipswich Town campaign in the 1980–1 season when, by common consent, the club was the leading footballing side in the British Isles. If we had finished winning nothing, people would have forgotten about us and I might have ended my association with the club. But we won the UEFA Cup. That was the highlight. There were a number of low points too.

Match 1 – Leicester City, AWAY, 16 August 1980

One of the last teams you want to start off against is a promoted side, because they are full of running and expectancy. Promoted sides usually do well in their opening matches as the enthusiasm developed in the promotion season is still there. If they don't do well at the start, they are dead.

Leicester's young side reflected the personality of their manager, Jock Wallace, who used to be my next-door neighbour for a while when we were players together at WBA. Jock is a tough, rugged, dour Scot and his players are hard to beat. We just managed it – 1–0 through a John Wark goal.

John Wark was to finish the season with thirty-six goals, a phenomenal total for a midfield player. He ranks as one of my best signings. John was recommended to me by my Scottish scout George Findlay. He was playing as a sweeper for Drumchapel Amateurs, the youth side that produced Asa Hartford and Archie Gemmill.

He was fifteen when he arrived at Portman Road for a trial, and both Bobby Ferguson and I liked him. I offered him a two-year contract, but he said he had promised to go back to Manchester City for more talks after a trial at Maine Road. His best friend, Alan Godfrey, had signed for City, and being a quiet, shy boy, he felt he would settle in better at a club where he knew someone. I tried to persuade him that he would have more chance of making the grade at a club like Ipswich which couldn't afford to go out and buy expensive players as Manchester City often did, but I was unsuccessful.

Two weeks later the phone went in my office and a Scots voice said: 'Could I speak to Mr Robson, please?' I thought it was John's father, but it was John himself. 'Do you remember me?' he asked. Remember? He was such a promising player that I couldn't forget. I had been hoping that something would go wrong at the City end.

'Do you still want me?' he said. I told him to catch a train the next day to Ipswich and we signed him straight away. Apparently Manchester City hadn't been back to him. His friend, Alan Godfrey, failed to make the grade there and is now driving a bus in Glasgow.

Match 2 – Brighton, HOME, 19 August

Another side that reflected the personality of the manager. Alan Mullery, who was then in charge, was a driving, forceful player who always played to his maximum, and his team was the same, full of solid types like Steve Foster, Mark Lawrenson and Mike Robinson. Mullery is a good talker and motivator, a man who gets players to play above themselves.

I knew that I had better players and that, providing we didn't do anything silly, we would win. We did, by 2–0, and it was a good start. Two wins from two lower section teams and everyone fit. At the end of the season Mullery left after a series of disputes with the board of directors. I was surprised he left. I thought he did a remarkable job in taking Brighton from the Third Division to the First but you rarely know what goes on within football clubs and how personal relationships change.

Match 3 – Stoke, AWAY, 23 August
This was a case of a point being dropped, because we led 2–1 until Stoke equalised near the end, and we had a good 'goal' disallowed. It was one of the few times I have gone into a referee's room to talk about an incident, but I felt it was justified.

Paul Mariner chased a through pass and as goalkeeper Peter Fox came out, he lobbed the ball over his head before crashing into the keeper. The referee gave an indirect free kick against Mariner for dangerous play. In my view, it was a disgraceful decision. Mariner had completed his kick before the collision, which was accidental, took place.

I waited until I had cooled down before going to see the referee. I didn't want a slanging match, and he put his view and I put mine. It was obvious we weren't going to agree. He saw the incident quite differently, but to me it was an example of how referees who haven't played the game at this level themselves can make decisions which cost professionals money, points and maybe even medals and cups.

I do not condone players acting like John McEnroe and disputing decisions. In fact, I do not tolerate blatant dissent at Ipswich. But there are times when a ludicrous decision is made, when I realise it is extremely hard to just stand there and say nothing.

I believe it should be made much easier for players to be encouraged to take courses and become qualified referees and after, say, one season in the Alliance League or the Football Combination, go straight on to the League list. It happens in cricket and many other sports, but football remains isolated as one of the few major sports where very few of the referees are ex-players.

The player knows who goes for the ball fairly and who doesn't, which player makes a 'back' when jumping for the ball and who is trying to kid the referee by feigning injury. When we have training matches I often ask players to take the whistle and some of them do a good job. It would not take long for them to become good referees but because it takes so many years for a referee to pass through the lower Leagues and eventually get on to the League list, hardly any players are interested in refereeing. I see it as an excellent way of staying in the game. If you ask players what they are going to do for a living after they retire, many don't know. They have made no plans. Refereeing would be an ideal employment, combined with running a small business, or taking a part-time job.

Some present-day referees say the most important factor in their job is handling people and that many players couldn't do that, but my reply to that is that it is not necessary for referees to enter into conversations with players. One of the best referees we had at Portman Road in my time was a Frenchman who didn't speak a word of English. His whistle did his speaking for him.

Match 4 – Middlesbrough, AWAY, Football League Cup second round, first leg, 26 August
The big thump as we came back to ground. Beaten 3–1 by John Neal's energetic, hard-working side, we were taught a lesson but this early in the season, it's not a bad idea to fail in these circumstances.

Match 5 – Everton, HOME, 30 August
We went to the top of the table with a 4–0 win, but it wasn't as easy as all that. My team talk, stressing the need to repair the damage at Ayresome Park, had been effective, but Gordon Lee's side came back well in the second half. I liked in particular their midfield player Steve McMahon. Wark's goal was tremendous – a volley from five feet off the ground. After the game some reporters tried to talk me into saying that Ipswich would stay on top for the rest of the season. I hedged. Forecasts have a habit of coming unstuck.

Match 6 – Middlesbrough, HOME, Football League Cup second round, second leg, 2 September
We squeezed through to the third round, winning 3–0. Paul Mariner scored twice on one of his better nights. Paul is a player who sometimes needs a stir. Most of us have our idiosyncrasies, and Paul is no different. When he is tough and competitive there is no better centre-forward in England. But when he sits back, as he does sometimes, and believes that skill is enough, his play deteriorates.

He can be complacent about what he is doing. Although I have to talk to him sometimes about attitude, we get on well. He doesn't bear any grudges.

We signed him for £120,000, plus John Peddelty and Terry Austin who were valued at £80,000, from Plymouth Argyle, in 1976, beating West Ham and WBA to his signature. It was a large sum for Ipswich to pay out at the time, but I thought it was worth it. I wasn't thinking of him as an England player at the time. I thought he was a good player who could adapt to First Division football.

Around that time I nearly bought Kevin Reeves from Bournemouth. We were selling David Johnson to Liverpool for £200,000 – good business as we bought him four years earlier in exchange for Rod Belfitt and £40,000 from Everton – and needed a First Division quality player as a replacement.

Reeves wasn't ready to go straight into the first team, or so I thought, and John Bond signed him for Norwich for £50,000, which was £10,000 more than I could have paid for him. I met Paul at the Great Western Hotel, and a delegation from WBA was there to see him on the same day. I was alone, whereas Johnny Giles, the Albion manager, had four other people with him. I said to Paul: 'If you come to us, you'll have only me to deal with. If you go to Albion, you will have to deal with all these people.'

Ron Greenwood, who was general manager of West Ham at this time, also offered £200,000. A point in my favour was that Paul liked country life and so did his wife, who is a schoolteacher. The idea of living in Constable country appealed to both of them. It was that factor, more than money, which swayed them.

Match 7 – Aston Villa, HOME, 6 September
The hardest match so far. We were slightly fortunate to win 1–0 against a very workmanlike side. At the time I couldn't see Villa being champions, although they were clearly going to run and run and keep running. It was reported that their players were on £250 a point, and that must have influenced their attitude. I believe players do think about money and what they are going to earn ... but not once the game starts.

Today's players are much more money-conscious than players in my day. Some of them are greedy and are becoming greedier every season. They want the manager to find ways of avoiding tax, and it can't be done. We are trying to spread their income over a period of years, as happens with authors and other big earners, but at present the Inland Revenue won't allow footballers to be treated like authors, boxers, pop stars and other performers who earn a lot of money in a short space of time. Most players have part of their salary paid into a pension fund which is payable from the age of thirty-five, but that only partly satisfies them. I feel more needs to be done to protect the long-term interests of players. We hear a lot about the big wage-earners, but we don't hear so much about players who have to retire from the game and have no training for another job.

In the main, that is the fault of the players for not preparing themselves for the second half of their lives, but I still think they could be advised to make better use of the money they earn while at their peak. You hear the players use the phrase 'secure my future', but no one can do that – not even millionaires.

By the end of the season, when Villa had clinched the title, I was pleased for their manager, Ron Saunders. He is a decent, straight, very reliable, almost predictable man, and those qualities are reflected in his team. He works hard, smiles rarely and usually manages to do the right thing. He prepared his team for the forty-two-match slog of the First Division in exactly the right way, and had few Cup distractions.

When he was manager of Norwich, I had little to do with him. He is not a man who needs to be on the telephone to his friends in the game all the time. His brief sojourn at Manchester City was one of the few bad periods of his managerial career. He fell foul of the extroverts on the Manchester City staff. It was they who got him out, not the directors.

Match 8 – Crystal Palace, AWAY, 13 September
Normally I get on well with Terry Venables, who was then the Palace manager, but this was one of the few occasions I have ever had words with him. We were sitting in our respective dug-outs when Eric Gates was flattened in the box and both Bobby Ferguson and I jumped up and shouted for a penalty.

Terry leaned out of his box and said: 'What are you talking about?' 'I'm not talking to you,' I replied. 'I'm talking to the ref.' I like Terry. He was a very intelligent player who knew the game, and that knowledge is coming out now that he is a manager. These touchline clashes between managers happen now and again, and I try to avoid them by sitting in the stand where I have a better view of the match.

Around this time Terry was under acute pressure. His team was bottom of the table and he was having problems with his directors. The nearer the manager is to the players, the more inclined he is to shout at them. At some grounds, particularly Anfield and Old Trafford, it is impossible to be heard unless the player is over the dug-out side of the pitch. Some managers will scream and shout for the full ninety minutes. One of the worst for making noise in my experience was Bob Stokoe, who has managed Charlton, Sunderland, Rochdale, Blackpool (twice) and Carlisle (twice) and has been in the game a long time.

Sometimes it is very necessary for the manager or coach to shout advice. In one game Kevin Beattie was lax and let an opponent in. I shouted at him but he didn't take any notice. Players can be like that. They hear you all right but carry on playing as though they can't hear you. I nailed Kevin afterwards. 'If you ignore me again, you're not going to be around this club much longer,' I told him.

We were leading 1–0 at Selhurst Park when I left late in the second half to catch a plane for Athens from London Airport. At five o'clock the scores came over the radio of the car as we were driving through Clapham. 'Crystal Palace 1 . . .' said the announcer, and I thought we had dropped a point. '. . . Ipswich 2.' That was a relief. It was a game we had to win if we were to keep the challenge going.

Match 9 – Aris Salonika, HOME, UEFA Cup first round, first leg, 17 September

I had seen little in Athens to make me think Aris Salonika would be too difficult opponents for us. The Greeks have some skilful players but their discipline lets them down. It did in this match, when they conceded three penalties, had one man sent off and three more cautioned by Portuguese referee Antonio Garrido. Their tackling was wild and, what was worse, it was carried out in dangerous areas, inside the box.

Gates was hacked down three times, and each time Wark scored from the spot. It has sometimes been claimed that Gates 'throws' himself, but I do not accept that. He is very adroit and clever when the ball is played up to him, and often a defender will commit himself and Gates goes over his foot. He gets a high proportion of our penalties and free kicks, but that is because he is always in dangerous positions and the ball is constantly being played to him when his back is to goal.

Our 5–1 victory meant that the tie was effectively over barring a miracle in Salonika two weeks later.

Match 10 – Coventry City, HOME, 20 September
We won 2–0 and played some beautiful football, but the 20,507 crowd dozed in the sunshine as though they were in Spain having an afternoon nap in front of the pool. I was so annoyed afterwards that I described them as 'zombies'. This was no sudden impulse. It was something I had been thinking about for some time.

The teams that win championships are usually supported by a noisy, enthusiastic crowd. There are two teams at a football club – the one out on the pitch and the other standing on the terraces and sitting in the stands. We weren't going to win the title with our team off the field dozing away and offering little encouragement. I had to stir them up, and this was my way of doing it.

It caused me a lot of problems. John Cobbold, a thoroughly nice, sensitive man who doesn't like aggro, thought my comments had been unnecessary but I told him this issue was a vital one for us. We had to make Portman Road a place where other teams didn't like coming to play – because of the quality of our football and because of the atmosphere. Liverpool's crowd was worth five points a season to them, I said. Ours was worth nothing.

In the next few days, the local newspaper was full of letters from angry supporters, and the newspaper itself criticised me. Perhaps I might have used a better word than 'zombies'. I did not want to hurt anyone's feelings and later said I was sorry if I had done so. But the message got across. By the next game supporters were wearing 'I am a Robson Zombie' badges and chanting 'Zombie' slogans. I had achieved my object. The crowd became more involved.

Match 11 – Norwich, HOME, League Cup third round, 23 September
There was a great atmosphere inside the ground, and the match, a 1–1 draw, was watched by our biggest crowd by far, 26,462. Randall Bevan, Director of Recreation in Ipswich, said: 'You were spot on. You've got what you wanted. It was a great bit of PR. Next time I want to get something across to the public, I'm coming to you for advice!'

Although the newspaper might have criticised me, I think I put my views over well on radio and TV. I see the public relations side as an important part of the manager's job. He has to sell his club and himself, and present the game in a good light. The arrival of local radio has helped football clubs. If you say something on the radio, it comes over as you say it, whereas sometimes with newspapers a comment is taken out of context and your views can be distorted.

The fact that Norwich held us to a draw was a tribute to their manager, John Bond, and the good work he put in at the club in his years at Carrow Road. On limited resources, he built a club worthy of competing with the best in the country. When he left, Norwich were relegated.

Justin Fashanu, the former Dr Barnardo boy, scored the goal. Big and strong, he is difficult to handle but is short on technique. He was to score another key goal against us later in the season.

Match 12 – Wolves, AWAY, 27 September
A game that emphasised the quality of our finishing. Paul Mariner and Alan Brazil scored two marvellous goals. We remained top of the table and had no senior players out of action with injuries. It had been a wonderful start to the season.

Match 13 – Aris Salonika, AWAY, UEFA Cup first round, second leg, 1 October
The trip to Greece should have been a pleasant break, but it became something of a nightmare. We were subject to tight security and there was an armoured car parked at the bottom of the road leading to our hotel high in the mountains overlooking the city. Armed police stood on duty in and around the hotel.

The local Press had given the Aris supporters the impression that their team had been cheated in the first leg. People went around saying 'Garrido' (the name of the referee in the first game) and drawing a forefinger across their throat. There was a hostile feeling in the air and we were glad to leave the place. As the coach drew away from the stadium after our 5–4 aggregate victory, a youth threw a stone through a window, narrowly missing George Burley.

We knew everything would be against us right from the start when Mick Mills cleared a shot off the line from a position a foot or two inside the pitch and the referee promptly signalled a goal. Later, Mick volleyed another corner away and that too was signalled as a goal – although the ball never crossed the line.

The pitch was full of ruts and potholes, almost like a park pitch. My players were holding themselves in check and playing without their usual competitiveness because of the danger of giving away free kicks and penalties. They were being taunted by opponents who spat in their faces. At 3–0 down in the sixty-fifth minute and with a volatile crowd of forty thousand baying for our blood, I thought we might be going out to one of the worst sides we have played in Europe, but Gates secured the game for us with a first-time shot on the turn in the seventy-third minute.

Match 14 – Leeds, HOME, 4 October
Allan Clarke's first match as manager of Leeds. He had ten men behind the ball and made it very frustrating for us. We were on our way to our first defeat until Arnold Muhren crossed and Warky took off to head a stunning equaliser. Clarkey and I had known each other well at Fulham, but we had no contact on this occasion. I didn't see him before the game, and afterwards he rushed off with his players.

Match 15 – Norwich, AWAY, League Cup third round replay, 8 October
This was one on TV and we showed the country what we could do. Muhren and Thijssen were brilliant, and Mariner scored twice in a 3–1 victory. I was beginning to worry, however, as I could see a fixture pile-up coming. The League Cup can be a nuisance for clubs who are in Europe. Some clubs, like Leeds, have been accused of 'taking a dive' in the League Cup so as not to overload their fixture list. I could never do that, but I must say I wouldn't be too unhappy at being knocked out. Since the winners now qualify for the UEFA Cup, the League Cup has become a more worthwhile competition, but it still lags well behind the FA Cup.

Match 16 – Liverpool, AWAY, 11 October
We gave Liverpool more problems than they gave us, and I realised then that we were capable of winning the championship. There was little between the sides in a 1–1 draw. Whichever club had fewer injuries could be expected to win, but as it turned out, both clubs were badly affected by injuries in the second half of the season and Aston Villa nipped in to beat both of us.

When I arrived at 10.45 to look at the pitch, big queues were forming outside the ground. The previous week I had letters from Ipswich fans complaining that they had arrived at Portman Road at just before seven for a seven-thirty start and hadn't been able to walk straight in! That was the difference between us, Liverpool could expect a regular turn-out of 45,000 plus (from a city population of 561,000, or one in twelve) whereas we had to be content with an average attendance of around 22,000. But considering the population of Ipswich was only 122,000, giving us a one in five ratio, our record bore comparison with that of any club in the country. Our trouble was that we suffered from lack of chimney pots!

Some critics had been suggesting that Liverpool were on the slide and would no longer be the force they were in the seventies. I could see no sign of a decline. They seem good for a few more years yet. They are self-perpetuating, success breeding more success.

Match 17 – Manchester United, HOME, 18 October
Before the home match against United the previous season, which we won 6–0, I had invited Dave Sexton and his assistant Tommy Cavanagh to my house to relax the night before the game. We smoked a cigar and chatted over old times. This time I invited Dave round again. 'You must be joking,' he said, 'You only did it last time to soften us up! You won't catch us falling for that again!'

Dave is a very mellow, quiet person and I like him a lot. He is one of the few managers who doesn't get irate when things go against him. If he suffers, he suffers inwardly.

This time United were much harder opponents, and we gave them a goal when Terry Butcher underhit a back pass and Steve Coppell scored. Paul Mariner scored for us in a 1–1 draw. The most disappointing feature was the injury to Frans Thijssen. He went off with a hamstring strain which was to keep him out for a month, except for an abortive return against WBA two weeks later which only aggravated the injury.

Sixteen matches without a serious injury isn't a bad record, but now the luck was starting to swing against us. In the next six weeks, eight players were to go down injured.

Match 18 – Bohemians of Prague, HOME, UEFA Cup second round, first leg, 22 October
The Czechs were a typically cautious Iron Curtain side with a sweeper system and only two players in attack. At half-time we hadn't scored and there were some anxious faces in the dressing-room. But often these home European matches are a matter of

patience. If you keep plugging away long enough, goals will eventually come, and that was what happened here with three coming in the final forty-two minutes without reply – a satisfactory lead to take back to Prague.

At the interval I said to the players we would have to play risk football and get round their defence more to whip in crosses. I told George Burley and Mick Mills to act as overlapping wingers. Crosses rained in, Warky scored twice and Beattie came on near the end to thunder in the third from a free kick.

Match 19 – Sunderland, AWAY, 25 October
I have always admired the Roker Park supporters and here was another illustration of their worth to the team. Ken Knighton's side came at us like raging lions, inspired by the fervour of the crowd. But goals from Muhren and Brazil soon sedated them. Mariner went off with a pulled hamstring and was to miss the next three games. Another worry.

Match 20 – Birmingham City, AWAY, League Cup fourth round, 28 October
No Mariner, no Thijssen and we lost 2–1. I wasn't sorry. You can't win every match, and as I said to Jim Smith, the Birmingham manager, an old friend from his days at Colchester: 'That will do you a lot of good.'

Match 21 – WBA, HOME, 1 November
Yet another injury. Paul Cooper went up for a cross and jarred his knee in a collision with Derek Monaghan. He carried on until half-time, when I asked the club doctor for an opinion about his chances of being able to continue. Cooper felt it was worth a try but with the Prague match four days away, I couldn't afford to take chances. We strapped the knee up and Cooper resumed, but only for a few minutes.

Allan Hunter used to be our stand-by goalkeeper and a fine goalkeeper he was. Now another centre-half, Russell Osman, had taken over the responsibility, and Russell did an excellent job without being under too much pressure. He likes playing in goal and often has practice sessions in training.

Dropping a point in a 0–0 draw was disappointing, and after taking only one point from Manchester United in the previous home match, it meant we had lost first place in the table.

Match 22 – Bohemians of Prague, AWAY, UEFA Cup second round, second leg, 5 November

Predictably, Cooper was out. He was to remain out of action for the next five matches, which was a blow because he was playing the best football of his career. We had a very capable deputy in little Laurie Sivell, who is one of the bravest goalkeepers in England. Without Cooper, Mariner or Thijssen, we knew it would be a test of our discipline and character, and in freezing cold conditions – the temperature was −16 °C – we just managed to hang on to go through on a 3–2 aggregate.

Beattie, the only player on the field wearing a short-sleeved shirt, did a fine job for us partnering Osman, and Butcher played at left-back. Bohemians were a different side to the one we played two weeks earlier, attacking in strength and pinning us in our own half. Antonin Panenka, their thirty-two-year-old schemer, was brilliant. Technically, the Czechs are fine players.

Match 23 – Southampton, AWAY, 8 November

After a punishing trip to Europe, you want a quiet, unexciting game. This was just the opposite. A 3–3 draw, it was a classic of a game and it had a bundle of controversy. In the second half Butcher tackled Mike Channon and was sent off. It was a hard tackle but he did go for the ball. Channon rolled over as he usually does in these situations.

Kevin Keegan burst on to the scene and told the referee to send Butcher off, which the referee proceeded to do. The referee may well have thought the incident was worth a sending-off, I don't know, but Keegan's action was inexcusable and I said so afterwards to the Press. Butcher is a mild mannered fellow. He's not one of the game's villains. Over the years we have had to work on his aggression because he tended to be too easy-going. A defender must have a little ruthlessness in him, otherwise he can't do his job properly.

Lawrie McMenemy tried to take the steam out of it in the Press room by saying what a marvellous match it was and why didn't the journalists concentrate on the football.

I was still seething in the directors' room afterwards, and when I saw Keegan talking to Ron Greenwood, I said to him: 'Listen, I've just had a go at you to the Press and I'm going to repeat what I said to your face. I don't think you needed to get involved in that incident. You helped get Butcher sent off.'

Keegan replied: 'He got himself sent off.'

'You ran thirty yards to go to the ref and speak to him,' I said. 'I don't think that's right. You're not the ref. Stay out of it.'

Keegan countered: 'I thought it was a bad tackle.' 'Well, let the people in charge deal with it,' I said.

I don't think that exchange will affect my relationship with him. I don't bear grudges and I remain an admirer of Keegan's. When I speak to my players, I use him as an example. 'He may be the richest player in the country but he's always the most enthusiastic still,' I tell them. 'His game is full of effort and you ought to strive to match him. He's prepared to stick his head in where it hurts and risk injury.'

Lawrie's signing of Keegan from Hamburg didn't quite work out as he planned in that season, although Southampton eventually got into Europe by finishing higher in the table than Nottingham Forest. After years without injury, Keegan suddenly developed a series of strains and couldn't perform with his customary verve. It was a shame. English football needed a fit Keegan that year.

Match 24 – Brighton, AWAY, 11 November
Butcher's suspension, plus the Cooper, Thijssen and Brazil injuries meant we had half a team out and we paid the penalty, losing our first League game 1–0 to a team we would normally expect to beat. We slipped to third place, but my confidence remained unshaken. At full strength, I knew we were a match for Liverpool, Villa or any other side in the country.

Allan Hunter, the thirty-four-year-old Irishman, came in to play his only game of the season as Butcher's replacement. I have often said that Hunter was my best signing at Ipswich. I bought him in 1971 from Blackburn Rovers for £60,000 plus Bobby Bell. I watched him three times before I made my mind up, and even then I wasn't sure I was doing the right thing. Ron Greenwood was in competition with me. He had watched him too and probably heard the same bad reports as I had heard.

When managers have fears about a transfer going wrong, they ring other managers and former managers to have their cards marked, and I spoke to Eddie Quigley, who managed Blackburn for a while and knew Hunter intimately.

'You'll have problems with him,' said Eddie. 'He's a bad trainer.' Quigley was right. I found it difficult to get Hunter moving in training. He would fight me all the way, and in the first two years I sent him off the training pitch countless times.

He was a moody Irishman, but those people who say players never change, or can't be changed, were wrong in his case because 'The Big Man' is now the most popular player in the club and has had more influence on Butcher, Osman and Beattie than anyone on the staff.

Match 25 – Leicester, HOME, 15 November
A poor game. We won 3–1 and Mich D'Avray, the South African, came on as substitute for the injured Gates to score a goal.

Match 26 – Nottingham Forest, AWAY, 22 November
We were fractionally the better side and won 2–1, a result which confirmed to me that we were still on course. I saw Brian Clough fleetingly. 'Well played,' he said. He is not a manager who socialises with the opposing manager before or after matches.

Match 27 – Widzew Lodz, HOME, UEFA Cup third round, first leg, 26 November
The Poles were quoted as favourites at this stage of the competition, and it was gratifying to beat them 5–0 in one of our outstanding performances of the season.

Before the kick-off Jacek Machcinski, the Polish coach, asked me if I would like to bet on the result. It may be normal practice for managers and coaches to bet on the outcome of games in Poland, but it doesn't happen in England! 'I think we will get a 2–2 draw,' he said, perhaps indicating the confidence he felt after seeing us play indifferently against Leicester.

'Yes, I'll bet,' I said. 'How much?' He replied: 'I have only Polish money.' Polish money was useless in Poland, let alone England, so the bet wasn't struck.

Even in the euphoria of a peak performance like this, there had to be a setback for our overall plans – the injury to Mick Mills which was to keep him out for a month. Mick tackled a Pole at the same time as Terry Butcher tackled him from the other side, and Terry's boot opened up a nasty-looking gash just above the ankle.

Match 28 – Manchester City, AWAY, 6 December
After a good match, a reaction tends to set in. You warn the players and everyone knows what is wanted, but somehow that extra bit of commitment is missing. We led through a splendid Muhren goal, but

City steamed into us in the second half and equalised. The dropped point meant we eased back to third place. John Bond was flattering afterwards. 'They're championship material,' he said.

Match 29 – Widzew Lodz, AWAY, UEFA Cup third round, second leg, 10 December

The newspapers were full of stories that the Russians were about to invade Poland. However much we want to keep politics out of sport, it is becoming more and more difficult to keep them apart. The club had to consult the Foreign Office for advice on whether it was safe to go to Lodz, Poland's second largest city, where there had been demonstrations by workers. The FO said their people in Warsaw saw no reason for us not to go, so we went.

Prague had been cold, but Lodz was worse. The snow was piled up in the streets and people walked with heads bowed and fur collars pulled up round their ears. The covering of snow on the pitch had been partly removed, leaving a mixture of snow and ice. In England the referee would have called it off without us having to leave the hotel.

But as the UEFA man said: 'I am sorry, but if we call it off we will not be able to play the game for another two months. And you have such a commanding lead!'

One of the Lodz officials smiled and said: 'Robin Cousins.' Even Robin Cousins would have struggled in the conditions. The dilemma I was in was simple: we should be able to defend a 5–0 lead, but was it fair to the players to risk it? Half a season's work could be thrown away. I decided to make no protest and get on with the job. If I let the players know I was worried, their feeling would be negative too, so I joked about it.

There was also a danger that players could pull muscles, so I made sure they prepared as well as possible to combat the extreme cold. Paul Mariner, for instance, had olive oil rubbed all over his body and wore tights under his track suit bottoms. He also wore two undershirts and a pair of gloves and padding on his arms.

The game went off without too many troubles, and it led me to think that maybe we postpone matches too readily in England. Players look for excuses. When there is snow about, everyone wants to stop playing, but in my playing days we played on snow.

Lodz won 1–0, but there was no danger of us going out. Within forty minutes of the finish we were on our way by coach to Warsaw

Airport. The coach ride proved to be more hazardous than playing on an icy pitch, with the vehicle sliding from side to side. Alongside the roadway there were a number of vehicles that had crashed.

Trevor Kirton, our kit man, who is known as 'Wheels', travelled independently with the kit in a van, and when we reached Warsaw, 'Wheels' hadn't arrived. The plane was waiting, we had a game against Liverpool three days later, and it was 11.30 at night. If we left before midnight, it would still be four a.m. before the players went to bed. I had to decide whether to fly off and leave him or stay on.

I decided my duty lay with the team and I deputed our interpreter to remain to aid Trevor. We were just saying our farewells when a coachload of musicians drew up – and out stepped 'Wheels'. He said the van had been driven by a lunatic and twice skidded off the road into a ditch. The first time he had dislocated a shoulder. Some by-standers pushed the van back on to the road and it set off again – only to crash again twenty kilometres further up the road. The impact put Trevor's shoulder back into place!

The van had to be abandoned, but luckily the coach with the musicians stopped and picked up Trevor and the gear. We had some Polish money left and I gave it to them. It was after four o'clock when the players reached their homes. Sixty hours later we were playing Liverpool, the best team in Europe.

Match 30 – Liverpool, HOME, 13 December
A 32,274 crowd, a great atmosphere ... and another 1–1 draw against the champions. Alan Brazil scored a marvellous goal and Liverpool came back well after having Johnston and Ian Rush injured. Sammy Lee went to centre-forward and surprised us – and probably Bob Paisley too.

Match 31 – Tottenham Hotspur, AWAY, 17 December
Our second defeat, 3–5, and a controversial one on a wild and stormy night. After a bad start, we were coming back into it at 3–3 when Eric Gates was sent off in the second half. Just before the incident, Tommy Eggleston had to go on to treat a player, and when he came back to the dug-out he said: 'That ref is shaking like a leaf. He's going to send someone off.'

The rain was lashing down and there had been one or two robust tackles. Steve Perryman, the Spurs captain, had been involved in one or two incidents, and I didn't like his attitude. Off the pitch he has the innocence of a choirboy, but on it he can be as hard as anyone when the boots are being raised.

Gates was in full flight when Graham Roberts tripped him, and Gates got up angrily and pushed out at Roberts. In no sense was it a punch, but the referee saw it as violent conduct and sent him off. I tore into Gates afterwards. 'You've cost us the game,' I said. 'You're the player who was fouled, yet you get sent off. We're not going to win the League if we're going to have players sent off for being unprofessional.'

Gates was just as angry. He blamed the referee. 'I should never have gone off,' he said. Keith Burkinshaw came into the Portakabin where we had changed – the new stand was just being started and there were no dressing-rooms – and sympathised with us. 'The decision was very unfair and very unkind,' he said. Osman and Wark had also been cautioned. John Martin, the referee from Alton, had a bad night and had cost us a point, maybe two. I couldn't say that in public, or to the players. In future, I told the players, you just have to walk away from trouble.

Match 32 – Birmingham City, AWAY, 20 December
Three great goals from Mariner, Wark and Brazil gave us a 3–1 win. Our percentage of goals scored per chance must be one of the highest in the Football League. We don't miss many and we don't miss extravagantly. It is no accident that so many go in. We have daily shooting practices and all the players join in. The game is about scoring, so one of our basic practice sessions is about mastering that most difficult part of the game.

Match 33 – Norwich City, HOME, 26 December
Ken Brown, newly promoted as manager, made Norwich fight hard, and it was a tight game which we won 2–0 to stay in third place. Ken is a nice man, down to earth and very sensible. He was number two to John Bond for many years and was clearly feeling his way as the boss. I thought he would make the grade and, after their initial reluctance, the Norwich directors felt the same way.

Match 34 – Arsenal, AWAY, 27 December
To win the title, I told the players, we have to take risks, even at places like Highbury. For too long the practice in many clubs is to go

for a win at home and try to hold on to a point away from home. It is a mean, niggardly way of winning the championship. The champions should be the best attacking side in the First Division, a team prepared to have a go and pit its skills against the other team, with class, hopefully, telling in the end. I believe in having a forward player as substitute, so if we go behind, we can put a player on who can put us back on terms and maybe even win the match. In forty-eight of the sixty-six matches in the 1980–1 season, we had an attacker as substitute.

This competitive 1–1 draw was an occasion where it worked. When we went behind I took off McCall and put on O'Callaghan, and Mariner scored an equaliser. Our courage was rewarded. It meant playing with only three at the back – Mills, Butcher and Osman – and it compelled the players to concentrate totally over the ninety minutes.

Don Howe and I always have good tussles. Under him, Arsenal deny the opposition space and counter-attack well. It is hard to beat Arsenal but we came close to it. It was a satisfying way to end the year, but there was no time to relax. The FA Cup third round draw paired us with Aston Villa, our rivals with Liverpool in the three-horse race for the League title.

Match 35 – Aston Villa, HOME, FA Cup third round, 3 January
The FA Cup is the New Year rejuvenator that rekindles interest and enthusiasm. All the clubs want a good Cup run, if only to bring in money. But to the players it's the glory scene. They're in the news and the talk is about Wembley. The FA Cup is the one part of our game that needs no alteration: it's perfect as it is. This year's was the hundredth, and that was an added incentive.

My players were slightly discouraged when they heard the draw. Villa were a team they wanted to avoid, along with Liverpool. I tried the psychological approach. 'How do you think the Villa players are feeling about coming to our place?' I asked them.

'Sick,' one of them replied. 'That's right,' I said. 'We've got the home advantage, and in the Cup that's what counts.' I wanted the players to think the positive thought, not the negative one.

In the end home advantage just swayed it and we won 1–0 through a Paul Mariner goal. I commiserated with Ron Saunders as we walked down the touchline at the end, saying: 'I know how you feel. At this stage home advantage gets you the result. Like last year, when we went to Everton and lost.'

Ron was downcast at the time, but this result was to clinch him the championship. It released Villa from any other commitments. All they had to concentrate on was the League, whereas we were in the FA Cup and the UEFA Cup as well as the League race.

Match 36 – Nottingham Forest, HOME, 10 January
It's not often your team does the double over Forest, but this was one of the rare occasions. We won three out of four meetings with them in the season, and Brian Clough said: 'I'm still not sure that they are a better side than us.' I didn't know what more we had to do to prove it!

We kept to the same tactics each time, because I believe a good side sticks to its basic principles. Liverpool have done that for years.

Match 37 – Birmingham City, HOME, 13 January
The tingle was coming back. We punched holes in Birmingham's defence and won 5–1 to go top of the table again. The pitch was covered with snow and the game was played with a red ball. Both the referee and Birmingham manager Jim Smith were keen to play, and Birmingham didn't try to put the boot in – which can often happen when a side is outclassed.

Match 38 – Everton, AWAY, 17 January
A heavy pitch and a tough, hard fought game. Gordon Lee, under pressure from his directors and fans, didn't want a repeat of the 4–0 beating at our place, so he kept it tight and the game ended in a 0–0 draw. We remained top.

Match 39 – Shrewsbury Town, AWAY, FA Cup fourth round, 24 January
These are the matches the FA Cup favourites, as we were at the time, hope to avoid – determined opposition, a cramped, packed little ground, and something missing in our attitude.

We could have lost, but scraped a replay in a 0–0 draw. The biggest disaster, though, was the loss of George Burley who went up for a high ball on his own and fell awkwardly, injuring his knee. We feared it might be a three-week job, but when the surgeon opened it up, he discovered that the lateral ligament had snapped and George was out for the rest of the year. Not many players return to one hundred per cent fitness after that injury but George was young, twenty-four, and had a lot of things working in his favour.

Match 40 – Shrewsbury Town, HOME, FA Cup fourth round replay, 27 January
Graham Turner's side dug in and battled hard again, but we were too good for them and won 3–0, sending them back home happy with some much-needed cash in their pockets.

Match 41 – Stoke City, HOME, 31 January
A great performance, and the score would have been more than 4–0 but for a splendid showing by their goalkeeper, Peter Fox. Alan Durban, Stoke's manager, was complimentary. He said we were a Rolls-Royce of a team.

Match 42 – Crystal Palace, HOME, 7 February
This was one of the times when I had to go steaming in at half-time and give the players a strong lecture.

I spared no one. I told them there were too complacent against a side that was bottom of the First Division, and no team had a divine right to beat another one, however poor that side might be. From 1–0 down, we swamped Palace with three goals in twenty minutes and then went back to sleep again. Mariner headed one the other way, past Paul Cooper, and it finished 3–2.

Palace's board had just changed, and a new team under Ron Noades were in the directors' box with their wives, making a lot of noise.

Match 43 – Charlton Athletic, HOME, FA Cup fifth round
Mike Bailey's side made it difficult for us without ever threatening Cooper's goal. I was impressed with their former England Youth forward Paul Walsh, but all his work was done outside the box. A comfortable 2–0 victory put us into the sixth round.

Match 44 – Middlesbrough, HOME, 17 February
A re-arranged League match. I had been angry when the original game was called off by the referee at breakfast time, and was happy we could fit it in before the inevitable fixture pile-up started. I told the players that a narrow 1–0 victory wasn't to be looked at negatively. To win the title, you often have to sneak 1–0 wins. Liverpool have been doing it for years.

Match 45 – Wolverhampton, HOME, 21 February
Our sixth successive home match and the sixth successive victory.
We seemed unstoppable. The score was 3–1 and could have been
far more. Paul Cooper even saved a penalty and John Richards was
so shocked he hit the rebound over the bar.

Match 46 – Coventry, AWAY, 28 February
The over-confidence which affected some players in the Crystal
Palace match was totally absent as we pounded to another big win,
this time 4–0. I suppose this period saw us at our peak. The machine
was running right and I didn't have to tinker with it. Management
was easy but I was alert for signs that things might be going amiss.

St Etienne, our opponents in the fourth round of the UEFA Cup,
had watched us four times and each time we won more handsomely
than the previous time. I think they overdid their scouting. You can
get the wrong understanding of a team's ability and transmit it to
your players.

Match 47 – St Etienne, AWAY, UEFA Cup fourth round, first leg, 4
March
They scored first but we didn't panic, even in front of an almost
hysterical forty-two thousand crowd. We came back to win 4–1 and
it was our greatest performance in Europe. Almost unbelievable.
There was no word of criticism I could utter.

We were in control nearly all the game and scored some amazing
goals. The crowd were stunned but they showed they appreciated
quality football when they applauded us off at the end. I was
ecstatic. Moments like these are rare in a manager's lifetime.

Match 48 – Nottingham Forest, AWAY, FA Cup sixth round, 7
March
Most of our hardest games were right after trips to Europe, but this
time it was less of a handicap because the players were still high on
the St Etienne result and needed no stimulus from me. Within
twelve minutes we were 2–0 up, which meant we had scored ten
goals in 192 minutes of football that week. That was how well we
were playing – ten goals and all away from home.

But near the end we were trailing 2–3 and I gambled by sending
on O'Callaghan for McCall, though Arnold Muhren was troubled
by a slight strain. It worked. Thijssen made it 3–3 and we had them
back at Portman Road. What a relief! The replay was scheduled for

Tuesday, but in view of our commitments and the punishing week we had had, I asked Cloughie to put it back a day to the Wednesday. 'Clear off,' he said. 'I want to play your lot again tomorrow – at 12.30 on the beach.'

He was less exuberant when I went to see him later to say good-bye. I knocked on his office door and heard a muted 'Come in.' I opened the door and stepped into a room that was pitch dark. For a moment I thought I was in the wrong room, but I could make out Clough's form lying on a sofa. Seated at a desk was Peter Taylor, and Kenny Burns, the club captain at the time, was sitting on a chair.

None of them was saying anything. They were just sitting there in the dark because there was no natural light in the office and the electric light was switched off. I was too surprised to say anything except 'See you on Tuesday.' That must have been their way of overcoming the disappointment of not going through to the semi-final of the Cup.

Not that I see much of Clough anyway. You never see him, or very rarely, before matches. He often marches in from the squash court, or wherever he goes, at 2.50 on match days and you never see him in the boardroom afterwards.

He is a one-off, a man who keeps very much to himself and doesn't share too much. He makes his exits and entrances in a hurry and has much less contact with his colleagues than any other manager.

He is never to be seen at meetings of FLESA, the managers' association, or at coaching courses. Nor does he watch other matches regularly like other managers. He leaves that to Taylor, his assistant, and they complement each other well. Taylor sizes up the players and recommends them, and Clough persuades his committee men – there are no directors as such at Forest – to lay out the cash. In the main, Clough and Taylor have bought well, but I felt they paid too much for Ian Wallace and Peter Ward.

Match 49 – Nottingham Forest, HOME, FA Cup sixth round replay, 10 March
Another great night for our fans. For twenty minutes Forest didn't allow us a kick while they over-ran us as no side has over-run us in my time at Portman Road. Wallace had the ball in the net but was rightly ruled off-side. We managed to hang on, showing immense character, and Muhren won it in the second half with a long-range volley. Right-footed too!

Match 50 – Tottenham Hotspur, HOME, 14 March

The bad feeling from the meeting at White Hart Lane three months earlier lingered on, and the game erupted into a nasty, unpleasant match which in my view brought no credit to the club that was to go on and win the FA Cup.

I have always had a high regard for Spurs and their way of playing football, and also for their manager, Keith Burkinshaw, but I considered that in this match they were over-physical, too frequently playing the man rather than the ball, and were intent on unsettling by unfair means a side that was after a unique Treble.

Being in three competitions confers no immunity against hard and fair tackling, but there was no excuse for some of the Spurs 'tackles'. The first offence, I admit readily, was committed by Osman when he dived in recklessly against Tony Galvin near the dug-outs and tripped him. It was a foul but not a bad one. Shortly afterwards, Don McAllister made no attempt to play the ball as he bundled into Mick Mills, and Mills went down in obvious pain.

Mick is no feigner of injury and I knew we had lost another full-back for a vital period of time. Tommy Eggleston said: 'He's dislocated a shoulder.' The injury was to keep him out of the next three matches, and I was most upset because it had been an uncalled-for assault. No sooner had O'Callaghan come on than he too was chopped down by Galvin right in front of the dug-out where I had come to see the extent of Mills's injury.

I jumped out to the side of the pitch and shouted to a linesman: 'Can't you see that?' I was incensed that such a blatant foul should go unpunished. The linesman was only a few yards away, having just examined O'Callaghan's studs.

Burkinshaw shouted at me: 'Ah, sit down.' I reacted angrily. 'Your players ought to behave themselves,' I said.

Later he was to make a cryptic remark to the Press about 'some people trying to get players sent off', but that had not been my intention. I was merely trying to direct the attention of the officials to one of several bad tackles which should have been checked, not ignored. Like mine, Burkinshaw's side was in the semi-finals of the FA Cup. Neither side wanted to have any of its players put out of action for the semi-finals in a month's time.

At half-time I said to the players: 'Let's take the heat out of this game by playing football. If they're going to continue dishing it out, I hope the referee has got the message by now.'

As I said to the Press, I don't know what was being said in the other dressing-room, but within seconds of the re-start Steve Perryman whacked Gates to the ground with one of the worst fouls of the game and left him with a cut on his leg.

Perryman has been a credit to the game, a thoroughbred player who has remained with Spurs all his career, a player a manager could build his side round. Neat and constructive, and a good tackler. But I hadn't liked his attitude in the first game when he had made some sinister comments. He had behaved like a ruffian. I don't know whether the captaincy had brought this streak out in him, but it seemed uncharacteristic. He was a nice boy off the pitch but a different kind of person on it. If anyone should be blamed for much of what went on in our two meetings that season, it was Steve Perryman, and that made me sad.

We won the match 3–0 to retain our lead in the championship, and even now I don't know why Spurs opted to play it that way. Both Burley and Mills were out of key matches and really it was a turning-point for us.

Match 51 – St Etienne, HOME, UEFA Cup fourth round, second leg, 18 March

With Kevin Beattie still troubled by his knee injury, I had to promote Kevin Steggles, a local player from the reserves, to take on Johnny Rep, the St Etienne Dutch World Cup striker. Kevin was twenty the day after the game and it was a nice birthday present for him. I told him two days before the match that he was in the side, so as not to put too much pressure on him.

A central defender, he slotted into the right-back position well and did a good job on Rep. The match was one of our quietest of the season, an anti-climax really once we went 5–1 up. We won 7–2 on aggregate, an overwhelming result against one of the best sides in Europe. It was encouraging that we had been able to play a low-key game and still win it easily. The critics were now beginning to assess our chances of winning the Treble. The pressure was mounting.

Match 52 – Manchester United, AWAY, 21 March

This is where it started to go wrong. We lost 2–1 on a pitch that was waterlogged in places. There were two inspections by the referee before the game was declared on. I attended the second, and he said: 'What do you think? You want to play, don't you?'

With our fixture situation I did want to play, but in normal circumstances I would have been happier with a postponement. It was one of those occasions where the managers could have tilted the referee towards calling it off, but Les Olive, the United secretary, also wanted the game to go ahead and, with neither side objecting, the referee allowed the gates to be opened.

Dave Sexton hadn't been on the winning side for weeks and needed a result. He got it, but that still didn't save him. We didn't play badly and I didn't see it as a foretaste of what was to come. Perhaps I should have.

Match 53 – Sunderland, HOME, 28 March
A 4–1 victory and a timely one. Muhren scored with one of the sweetest free kicks I have seen.

Match 54 – Leeds, AWAY, 31 March
An awful night. After our players had warmed up there was a knock at our dressing-room door at 7.25 and a man popped his head in and said: 'The game has been put back until 7.45.' I was annoyed, because you like to know these things early to enable you to change your plans. 'Does Allan Clarke know?' I asked pointedly. 'Yes,' said the man. 'You bet he does,' I said.

I went to see the referee and asked him what it was all about. 'They can't get the crowd in,' he said. 'They've turned up late and they're all trying to get in at once.'

That wasn't our fault. I thought it was unfair that we had been told so late, especially as Leeds must have known much earlier. My players were moaning, and were in the wrong frame of mind when the game eventually started.

Paul Hart, normally a centre-half, was moved into attack, and as Paul Cooper came out to hold a cross, with Osman and Butcher challenging Hart, the referee awarded a penalty. At worst, it was obstruction. That goal set us on the way to a 3–0 defeat, our heaviest defeat of the season. The players were very downhearted.

Match 55 – WBA, AWAY, 4 April
This was the second match of a crucial period of thirty-three days when we were scheduled to play ten games. It was crazy, but we had to do it if we were going to win all three trophies, or two, or even just one. It was the price of success.

I decided to miss the trip to the Hawthorns and leave Bobby

Ferguson to take charge while I flew to Karlsruhe in West Germany to watch FC Cologne, our opponents in the semi-final of the UEFA Cup. We hired a four-seater plane for £270, and my nineteen-year-old son Mark accompanied me. Soon he was probably wishing he had stayed behind. The weather was bad, with low cloud, and the forecast was that there would be no improvement. Once we were in the air it was impossible to see anything. The pilot, an experienced man, used the beacon-to-beacon system of navigation.

As we neared Karlsruhe, the pilot said: 'The airport there is closed. We'll have to try Stuttgart.' A few minutes later he reported: 'Stuttgart is closed as well. We'll have to head back towards France and see if it is any better there.'

It is an eerie, frightening feeling being four thousand feet above sea level and not knowing if you will set foot on land again. I had chosen a small plane from Southend because it was more convenient than driving to London to fly to one of the major cities by one of the big airlines. Now I wished I had been more patient.

We closed in on Strasbourg, the nearest airport in France, but when we got over the runway the pilot couldn't see it. We came in a second time and again the fog was too dense. Apparently the regulations say that twice is enough and after two attempts another airport has to be found. I became more and more nervous, thinking to myself, 'For goodness sake let's get down somewhere.'

As the pilot came in for the final approach, a gap suddenly appeared and we could see the landing strip and the lights from an altitude of 180 feet. I have never been more relieved. We were able to land safely, thanks to the skill of the pilot.

The match, in which Tony Woodcock was sent off rather unluckily, had become very unimportant. The next problem was getting home. We arrived back at Strasbourg from Karlsruhe by taxi at 7.30, and the weather was still bad, with the fog closing in again.

Apprehensively, we got into the plane, the pilot sorted out his flight path and we prepared to take off. But after talking to the tower, the pilot said: 'Gentlemen, it's not on.'

'That's great,' I said. 'I don't want to go through that again.' We stayed the night. The next morning the fog had cleared and we were able to make the trip without hindrance. I rang Elsie and she told me that WBA won 3–1, but Bobby Ferguson said we had played well. Ominously, we had been knocked off the top by Villa and were now second after two successive defeats.

Match 56 – Cologne, HOME, UEFA Cup semi-final, first leg, 8 April

Our first Euro semi-final, and we won 1–0, though it could have been 3–0. John Wark headed the goal, maintaining his remarkable record in the competition. Cologne were unadventurous and I felt they weren't good enough to stop us reaching the final. Not that we had any time to think of the final, because in three days we faced Manchester City in the semi-final of the FA Cup.

Match 57 – Manchester City, at Villa Park, FA Cup semi-final, 11 April

We stayed at a hotel outside Birmingham, and some of the players were woken in the night by ducks quacking outside. The football manager is always searching for quiet hotels where his players can rest before important games, but sometimes even the quietest of places can be disturbing, and so it proved this time.

There was a more upsetting happening later at lunch, when we were half-way through out pre-match meal. It is a tense time, particularly when the game is a semi-final and the players know they are ninety minutes away from Wembley and all that that means.

The hotel manager came into our room and asked us to leave our bedrooms because he had guests waiting to take them. It was a most ill-timed request, and I said: 'Can't you wait until we are finished?'

'No,' he said. 'We need the rooms now.' I was incensed and said: 'We're playing in the semi-final of the Cup in a few hours. You don't have people actually wanting to use the rooms at this minute, do you?' He said he did.

We were supposed to be staying at this hotel the following Monday before our re-arranged League fixture against Aston Villa at Villa Park, but I told him to cancel our reservation. I believe this extraordinary saga affected my players and may have contributed to their 1–0 defeat at the hands of John Bond's team.

Footballers are creatures of habit. They like to follow a familiar routine, and if their routine is upset, it distracts them. There were no other obvious reasons for our poor performance. I didn't think nerves were to blame, as we had just played a semi-final and won it. We were a more experienced side than City, and some of our more experienced players like Mariner, Mills and Thijssen were among those who didn't do their talents justice.

As extra time loomed, I thought that was just what we didn't need, with the Aston Villa game only three days away. The extra thirty minutes would take a higher toll of my players, and so it proved. The match was won when Paul Power, the City captain, bent a free kick past Cooper. To compound our miserable day, Kevin Beattie broke his arm and was out for the rest of the season – just when we needed him most.

It was a morbid ride home in the coach, with players sitting in silence looking out the windows at the waving fans who overtook us or were overtaken. I felt sorry for the fans. They had spent a lot of money and now weren't going to Wembley.

Match 58 – Aston Villa, AWAY, 14 April

One thing about a crowded fixture list: there is no time to mope about defeats. We had a long talk on the Monday morning, and I stressed the positive side and the fact that we were still well placed to win two out of three. Our pattern of play had suffered at Villa Park, and we had to go back to the style which had got us this far.

None of the critics gave us a chance against Villa. Nor did many of the 47,495 spectators. The pressure was off us, and we responded with a 2–1 victory which shocked everyone and showed the footballing world what we could do when we were supposedly down. As I shook hands with a disappointed Ron Saunders, he said: 'We gave you two.' I have never played against his teams when they haven't given us goals!

Match 59 – Arsenal, HOME, 18 April

Easter is traditionally the time when championships are won and lost, and this year was no exception. I tried to make our task a little easier by seeking a postponement of the following Monday's game at Norwich, but Ken Brown declined, and in his position I would have done the same.

Arsenal, awkward as ever, beat us 2–0. We missed Thijssen's influence. He was still out with a hamstring. Brian Talbot, whom I had sold to Terry Neill, battled hard to get the better of his old club, as he always does, and new signing Peter Nicholas had a good début. Arsenal were fresher. They were like dogs after a rabbit – and a tired-looking rabbit at that. Another worry was an injury to Eric Gates, but as I told the players: 'We're not finished yet.'

Match 60 – Norwich, AWAY, 20 April

No Burley, Beattie, Mariner, Gates or Thijssen. We had only half a team, and we gave the match to Norwich with a goal scored by Justin

Fashanu. This infuriated me because of the unprofessional attitude of our defenders at the end of a season when they had played so brilliantly.

Fashanu went up the left, and as he cut in we had five men in the box to their none. With no one to pass to, Fashanu ought not to have been a threat. But to my astonishment, Cooper came racing out of goal to throw himself at Fashanu, and Justin put the ball past him on the near post. Cooper had had a wonderful season and deserved every praise, but he knew that was bad keeping and I told him so in the dressing-room.

It was the lowest hour of my managerial career. In nine days we were out of the FA Cup and the League championship race, and I told the Press: 'We lost the title here today.' In fact, it was still possible to pip Villa if we won our remaining three matches, against Manchester City, Middlesbrough and Southampton, and if Villa lost their final game at Arsenal. I found myself talking about leaving the club and starting again elsewhere, but qualified it by adding: 'If we win the UEFA Cup I might feel differently.'

Mick Mills said after the Final that he felt that statement put pressure on the players. Too right it did. I did that calculatingly, because I wanted them to feel pressure. I wanted them to feel they *had* to win the UEFA Cup. But whether I remained or went had nothing to do with him. Players think they are under pressure, but they aren't. It is managers who are under the real pressure. If players lose a game or two they are still in a job, but for managers it can mean the sack.

Match 61 – Cologne, AWAY, UEFA Cup semi-final, second leg, 22 April

Thijssen felt he could play, but Mariner's Achilles tendon strain – a wear and tear injury caused by playing too many games in too short a time – was still worrying him.

I took Mariner aside and told him he would have to play. Usually I leave it to the player's own judgement, but this time it was too important a game for the club. I was literally forcing him to play. Fortunately he agreed. Cooper had taken his rollicking well and put on a great display. He was dominant in the air and finished up as my man of the match. When Terry Butcher headed the sixty-fourth-minute goal, which gave us a 2–0 aggregate, it was a superb feeling, making up for the acute depression I had felt forty-eight hours earlier.

March 62 – Manchester City, HOME, 25 April
Too late, we beat John Bond's team 1–0 with a scintillating
performance which rejuvenated the crowd. Georg Kessler, manager of our UEFA Cup opponents AZ Alkmaar, came into the
boardroom with his notebook afterwards and I told him: 'That was
our reserve team.' Both Thijssen and Mariner were resting, and
Burley and Beattie were still out.

Match 63 – Middlesbrough, AWAY, 2 May
At half-time it was still going well. We were 1–0 up and in control.
Villa were losing at Arsenal. Miraculously we were back in with a
chance of taking the title.

But in the second half the mood of the players changed, and I
didn't know why. Sitting up in the stand, I felt like shaking them by
the throat. It was roller-coaster time, and we were crashing back
towards the ground. I felt powerless.

Osman and Steggles failed to mark Bosco Jankovic, Boro's
Yugoslav centre-forward, and he headed the equaliser. Then near
the end Mills was slow to challenge for a cross and Jankovic headed
in the winner.

I couldn't believe it. Everything went right for us at Highbury,
where Villa lost 2–0, yet we disintegrated. I had to be careful what I
said. To go storming into the dressing-room would be like kicking a
wounded dog, especially as we still had the UEFA Cup final first leg
to play the following Wednesday.

Match 64 – AZ 67 Alkmaar, HOME, UEFA Cup Final, first leg, 6
May
The previous Sunday I flew to Rotterdam to watch AZ beat
Feyenoord 5–1. AZ convinced me that they were the best side in
the competition and we would have to play well to beat them. Once
again, it was a scary ride. Bobby Ferguson and I took off on a grass
strip at Elmsett in a single-engined plane which bounced around in
the air.

The journey back was marginally worse as we crossed the North
Sea. On our arrival, we were invited into the control tower at
Southend for a cup of tea, and the staff there were most surprised to
learn that we had not flown down the French coast and taken the
shortest possible route across the Channel.

'Anything could have happened to a small one-engined plane in this wind,' said one of the staff. 'Were you wearing a life jacket?' I said we weren't. 'You must be crazy,' he said.

On the Monday I had a talk with the players, and they accepted blame for their abysmal second-half performance at Middlesbrough. I think it helped put them in the right frame of mind to take on AZ.

Eric Gates was the key man in our tactical plan. Kessler put full-back van der Meer on him in the second half, and he couldn't handle him. The amazing Wark converted a penalty in the twenty-eighth minute to confirm his reputation as one of the most assured penalty-takers of recent years, and when Thijssen added a second in the forty-sixth minute, I knew we were on our way and that I would be staying at the club.

A third goal from Mariner in the fifty-sixth minute gave us a 3–0 lead to take to Amsterdam two weeks later ... and we were to need it!

Match 65 – Southampton, HOME, 13 May

An unreal evening. With Villa having already won the title there was no pressure on us, while Southampton had to win to qualify for the following season's UEFA Cup at the expense of Nottingham Forest. We were so slack in the opening twenty minutes that Saints scored three times, two goals coming from the highly promising Steve Moran.

'If you play like that in the Amsterdam game, you won't win the UEFA Cup,' I said. We tightened up in the second half and scored twice to go down 2–3. But it was still very unsatisfactory. Potential season-ticket buyers judge a team partly on its last game, and this one had been a let-down for the public.

Match 66 – AZ 67 Alkmaar, AWAY, UEFA Cup Final, second leg, 20 May

Lawrie McMenemy had finally decided to stay with Southampton, so the questions about the job at Manchester United were now coming my way. I said I had not been approached and wouldn't make any decision about my future until after the second leg of the UEFA Cup.

All the players were fit and there were no problems on that score. Once again, however, bad luck continued to afflict our season, because just before the coach was due to leave the hotel for the

Olympic Stadium, four players, Mills, Cooper, Brazil and Gates, were trapped in a lift.

The temperature outside was in the eighties, and they spent an exhausting twenty minutes in a confined space before the lift was reactivated. Hardly ideal preparation for the most important game of a long season!

The departure was delayed while the four players had a quick shower and a change of clothing. As I expected, AZ played with only two defenders marking Mariner and Brazil, and attacked with eight men. They overcame the blow of conceding a fourth-minute goal to Thijssen and came back so devastatingly that for a time we were under siege. AZ won 4–2, but lost 5–4 on aggregate, and the season had been worthwhile after all. Our football would be remembered.

Seventeen

Staying On

The caller wouldn't give his name. He spoke in a northern accent and sounded elderly. 'In a few days' time a certain northern club will be without a manager and the job will be offered to you,' he said. He rang off, and when I told Elsie, she said: 'It's a hoax.' I thought of the northern clubs who might be sacking their manager and came to the conclusion it was Manchester City.

Ipswich had just beaten Bristol City 3–0 in the first leg of the FA Youth Cup Final at the end of the 1972–3 season, and we were to draw the second leg 1–1 at Ashton Gate. The upheaval at the club had ended and some promising young players were coming through from the youth policy. It was the first time Ipswich had been success-ful in the Youth Cup. Hardly a time, I felt, to be thinking about leaving.

But I wasn't under contract at Ipswich, and there was my family to consider. A few days later it was reported that Harry Catterick had quit at Everton because of illness. So it was Everton! I was excited. Everton always appealed to me as one of the big clubs in British football. I loved going there for matches.

'Deep Throat' was soon on the phone again. 'They want to set up a meeting with you,' he said. But before a meeting could be arranged, John Cobbold, the Ipswich chairman, heard about the speculation. 'Look,' he said. 'We don't want to lose you. You don't want to go, do you?'

'Not really,' I said. 'But I have to consider it.' 'We'll give you more security than any club manager in the country,' said Mr John. 'What about a ten-year contract at £10,000 a year?' It was the first ten-year contract to be offered in the Football League, and I was delighted to accept it.

When we stepped off the train on the return trip from Bristol City, some of the first-team players were waiting for me, including Dave

Johnson, whom I had just signed from Everton. 'You're not going to walk out on me, are you?' he said. 'Don't go!' I told him I was staying.

When I first met the directors of Ipswich Town in 1969 I told them I was a person who didn't like hopping about from club to club. I had had two clubs in eighteen years and preferred to put down roots. 'I hope to be with you a long time,' I said.

If a manager has success, he is in demand, and in my years at Ipswich I was continually being put in the quandary of having to decide whether to stay or go somewhere else and earn much more money. Each time I stayed, but it caused me much agony of mind. There are basically two types of manager. The first is the man who likes to go to a big city club where there is plenty of money. He is the front-of-house man, the manager who likes the limelight and the glamour of a big club.

His judgement of players has to be right because he is spending a lot of money. But most of his other roles are delegated. He has coaches to do the coaching, directors and administrators to do the cash side of it, and scouts to do the scouting. Ron Atkinson is one of the best known of this type, a man with box office appeal, a man with a certain amount of charisma.

He has done a good job at Old Trafford and has shown he can cope with the pressure. He was made for the job. He has probably paid more money for his players than he should have done, but that wasn't his fault. United wanted star names and they had to pay the price.

Judging by the salary United paid Dave Sexton, which I learned was one of the lowest in the First Division, the club weren't as extravagant in paying their manager as they were in paying for new players. But that wasn't a factor when Martin Edwards, the Manchester United chairman, rang and offered me the post of United manager in May 1981. Lawrie McMenemy was the first choice and had turned it down. Edwards explained that he didn't want any more bad publicity and requested that I keep our conversation private. He said he couldn't afford another public rebuff.

I told him I felt the same way as Lawrie. If Ipswich hadn't won the UEFA Cup perhaps my answer might have been more encouraging, but I had had an offer from Sunderland at the same time and that had more appeal to me than the Manchester United offer. I couldn't see myself as a media manager in daily competition for column inches with John Bond, who had not long previously joined

Manchester City. I felt I could take the pressure but my training had equipped me for a different type of management – the second kind, where the manager is primarily a coach in a club which cannot afford to go out and buy million-pound players.

This kind of manager is judged by what he does over a period of time – building up a youth policy, producing mainly his own players and buying others for moderate sums. He is rated according to where the club stands when he left it compared to where it was when he arrived. If he has lifted it to a higher position, then he is a success. His job is to take over the running of the whole club and instil discipline and motivation.

Something more than discipline and motivation were needed at Derby County in October 1973, when Brian Clough and Peter Taylor left the club in a welter of controversy and Sam Longson, the man who forced them out, rang me and offered me the job. The club was a cauldron, with players taking the side of Clough and Taylor and police needing to be called to remove angry supporters.

I first met Sam a couple of years before and had a liking for him. He was a bluff Midlands businessman who had a way of coming straight to the point. 'We need you up here quick, laddie,' he said. 'Money is no object. We'll beat any other offer you're getting.'

Clough won the League title in 1971–2 and had transformed Derby into a top club with average home attendances of 30,000. He made some tremendous buys, and it was very clear that the fans were on his side. The new manager had that to contend with and also the political manoeuvrings in the background.

To quell the unrest, Longson needed to make an appointment within hours, and I was his first choice. That Saturday Ipswich were playing Arsenal and I took the opportunity to ask Bertie Mee, Arsenal's manager, for advice. I knew Bertie well and had always liked him. He was a sensible man who had achieved the highest honours in the game. If anyone was worth listening to, it was him.

'You will be walking into a minefield,' he said. 'There's such a lot of controversy going on there. It's too hot. You will be left holding the baby.' I decided that was good advice and rang Sam Longson next day to turn down his offer. He sounded disappointed. Not long afterwards he gave the job to Dave Mackay, Derby's former captain, who was managing Second Division Nottingham Forest with little success at the time.

David was a great player, a gritty, barrel-chested figure who inspired the men around him. But great players don't always make great managers, and that was so in his case. He led Derby to another championship in 1974–5 with the very good side Clough left behind, but the club went downhill fast.

He took over a Rolls-Royce and it kept going until it needed some attention, but when that happened he was found wanting. By strength of personality he managed to win over the players at first, but there is more to management than a strong personality. The shadow of Clough was always behind him. I don't believe in too many of the things Clough does, but no one can deny him his extraordinary record as a manager.

In 1974 there was another drama, with a big club wanting me, when Leeds asked me to succeed Don Revie, who had been appointed Sir Alf Ramsey's successor as England manager.

I was in my office one day when the switchboard girl said: 'There's someone from the West Riding Referees' Society on the line for you.' I was tempted to tell her not to put him on. Referees' societies usually want managers to address their meetings, and it is not always convenient.

'Okay, put him on,' I said. I recognised the voice immediately. It was Tony Collins, one of Revie's assistants at Leeds. 'Don wants to talk to you,' he said. 'Why are you posing as someone from the Referees' Society?' I asked. 'We want to go about it discreetly,' he said.

Revie came on the line. 'I want you to come to Leeds,' he said. 'You can't turn it down. They're the best club in the country, the best squad of players, the best training facilities. It's made for you. It's a nice, clean tidy club with no loopholes.

'All it needs is for someone to keep it going. I've recommended you to the board. When can you come? I can get you £25,000 a year. They'll offer you £20,000, but don't take it. I'll get you £25,000.'

I had always admired Revie as a manager. He had taken the club and built it up into an outfit that was the envy of the Football League. The names reeled off the tongue – Sprake, Reaney, Cooper, Bremner, Charlton, Hunter, Lorimer, Giles, Clarke, Jones and Eddie Gray. The team picked itself. But there was something about the club I didn't fancy. Too many players were close to or over thirty and would need replacing. It was Don Revie's team. He had built up a family atmosphere there and I could foresee that the new man would have problems stamping his personality on the club.

Nevertheless, I was only earning £10,000 a year at Portman Road and even £20,000 would be a tempting inducement, let alone

£25,000 plus all the other perks. Perhaps it was time I moved on, I thought. I decided I would see Manny Cussins, the Leeds chairman, and his directors, and a meeting was fixed at the Royal Garden Hotel in London. They were very nice about it and, as Revie had predicted, they offered £20,000. They said they wanted someone who commanded respect in the game, someone like Don Revie. I told them I would think about it and give them my reply within forty-eight hours.

When I rang to say I was staying at Ipswich, Manny Cussins said: 'Don Revie will be very disappointed.' I was under contract to Ipswich but never spoke to John Cobbold about Leeds and although the news broke in the newspapers, he never asked me what was happening. That was his style when he was chairman: he never interfered.

It was the directors rather than Revie who eventually made the decision to appoint Clough and brought him to Elland Road from Brighton. Clough took over and moved in like a whirlwind. But he under-estimated the personalities of some of the senior Leeds players, experienced internationals like Bremner, Hunter and Clarke. They resented his comment that he would make Leeds a better team, and he finished up being broken by them. Joining Leeds was one of the few mistakes in his chequered career. Within forty-four days he was out, and Jimmy Armfield, a vastly different personality, took over.

Jimmy was a quiet man, a former captain of England with whom I had played many times. He was one of the first full-backs to overlap, a cultured, intelligent player, but I felt he handicapped himself severely while at Leeds by continuing to live in Blackpool. In management, you have to live close to the job. You can't be a commuter.

I was conscious at this time that some people in football were saying I was frightened of joining a big club. I was talked of as being someone whose style of management suited him to a smaller, less ambitious, less demanding club. That did not worry me. You do what you think is right in life. It is your decision, and your quality and style of life depends on your needs and ambitions. My ambition was to build the finest club in the country, and I felt I was in the process of doing that at Ipswich. In 1975 we weren't far off doing the Double. We beat Leeds in the FA Cup. We were a big club in all but name. I had created that largely through my own efforts. Ipswich had no tradition like Manchester United or Liverpool. But we were building a tradition and I found that exciting and stimulating, much more so than the prospect of doubling my salary.

Being successful meant the offers kept coming in, on average one a year. I was holidaying with the club in Martinique in 1975 when I was tapped by Lord Westwood, who was then President of the Football League. He wanted to know if I was interested in taking over at St James's Park, and I replied that as a Newcastle supporter in my youth, the idea did interest me to a certain extent.

He asked me to call John Cobbold and seek his permission to talk officially with Newcastle. I told him I thought he should have done that himself but he didn't seem to want to face the ordeal. I saw no point in continuing the discussion and told him so.

In 1976 it was the turn of 'Deep Throat' again. The phone rang at home, and a voice which I recognised instantly said: 'A club in the North-West will be terminating the contract of its manager soon. Are you interested in the job?' I said: 'I know you. It's Everton.'

'That's right,' he said. 'How do you feel about it?' 'I keep getting these offers,' I said. 'Soon, I'll have to decide once and for all whether to take one or stay at Ipswich.'

'It's an offer you can't refuse,' he replied. Over the next few days I thought this might be the time to move on. I had been at Ipswich eight years and though the team was doing well, that was a long time for a manager to stay at one club. Everton caught me at a vulnerable time.

Early in January 1977, one of their directors phoned and said John Moores, the head of Littlewood Pools and former chairman of Everton, wanted to see me. I drove to his home in Formby, Lancashire, an unpretentious old house, and talked with him over a light lunch. His deep love of Everton Football Club soon came over in our conversation. He convinced me that I could make Everton a great club again, able to compete with Liverpool on equal terms, and he was so persuasive that I was veering towards the idea that perhaps this could be the time to change clubs. He seemed a nice old man. I liked him a lot.

'If you come, I know it will be hard for you to tell John and Patrick Cobbold,' he said. 'I suggest you come up here, sign a contract, and I will ring them and discuss a settlement.' The Ipswich directors had a great rapport with the Everton directors and they always had lunch together before matches. There was an affinity between the clubs and I didn't want to see that broken.

I told Mr Moores that I wasn't happy with his plan. 'That's not the way I want to do it,' I said. 'I want to tell them myself. I want to be fair with them.' That was the only thing that disturbed me about my meeting with Mr Moores. I knew it went on in managerial changes but I didn't want it to happen with me.

Elsie agreed with me that I should take the Everton job, because it was good for my career and it was an offer that was unprecedented in English football at the time. The starting salary in a ten-year contract was £25,000 plus an £8,000 bonus. In addition there were some extras like £10,000 for winning the League Championship, £10,000 for the FA Cup, £20,000 for the European Cup, £15,000 for the European Cup Winners' Cup, £12,000 for the UEFA Cup and £10,000 for the Football League Cup.

Everton agreed to buy my house near Ipswich and offer me a one hundred per cent interest-free loan to buy a house in the Liverpool area. They also agreed to pay me the bonus I would have received had I stayed on at Ipswich. We finished third that season, so I would have qualified for a bonus of £4,000 if the Everton scale had applied.

Everton had prepared a letter for me to sign, addressed to the Ipswich directors. It said: 'I have to advise you that after very careful consideration I have decided to resign as manager of Ipswich from this weekend. An opportunity has arisen which I am convinced will result in an improvement of my present and future position and I have agreed to join Everton as their manager.

'I have made this decision only after a very thorough review of the future of my family and myself, and I very much regret that this can cause Ipswich some disturbance. I leave the club in a sound and strong position and I wish them well for the future.

'I hope you will not think too harshly of me and will remember that in my eight years with Ipswich I have brought the club many successes, and that I will leave the club in a far better position than it was in when I took over.

'May I add my thanks to you and all the directors for their help and guidance which have made my years at Ipswich very happy ones, which I will always look back upon with pleasure.'

This letter was handed to me by one of the Everton directors at a secret meeting at the Newport Pagnell service station. However, I told him that I didn't want to be party to sending such a letter. I told him I would see John and Patrick Cobbold myself in the morning. We shook hands on the deal. Except for the formality of telling the

Ipswich Board, I was now boss of Everton Football Club. I drove home and told Elsie that we would be moving house again.

Everton wanted to send a chauffeur-driven car to Portman Road on Monday morning to pick me up to take me to Liverpool. They wanted me out of town as quickly as possible. I suggested a compromise: I would meet the car at the Post House Hotel on the outskirts of Ipswich. That was a more diplomatic way of handling it.

That morning I was up soon after day-break. I went to the door to collect the newspapers and the mail. I turned to the back page of the *Daily Express*. There was a streamer headline: 'BOBBY ROBSON GOES TO EVERTON.' The story was all there. I couldn't believe it. I hadn't yet told the Ipswich directors, and here it was in a newspaper.

I felt very bitter and very angry. The contract hadn't been signed, yet they released the news. They had let me down badly. In a few seconds my mind was made up. I wouldn't go to Everton. I would stay at Ipswich. If they could behave like this over their first dealings with me, then what might happen in the future? I couldn't trust them.

After breakfast, I rang the Tolly Cobbold brewery and asked to speak to Mr John. 'You've probably read the newspaper, and I'd like to come and see you about it,' I said. He asked me to come down to the brewery. He sounded matter-of-fact, and not agitated as he might have been.

We could have parted as friends. Now there was a bad taste. John and Patrick were both there. 'It's true what you've read in the papers, except that I'm not going,' I said. 'If you still want me, I'm happy to stay. But if you feel that you don't want me to after this – well, I'll go.

'It was an offer I couldn't refuse, but it was dependent on seeing you this morning. Now the story has broken, it's all off as far as I'm concerned, and if you want me, I'll stay.'

Patrick Cobbold, who by then had taken over from John as chairman, didn't seem upset. 'Fine,' he said. 'That's the best news I have heard all day.' He said the club wouldn't release me from my contract anyway so there was no point in talking about my departure. The meeting lasted thirty minutes and couldn't have been more amicable.

Back at the ground, a small delegation of players was waiting for me. They told me that if I left, they would all ask for transfers. I told them I was staying. I rang the Everton director and told him the deal was off because I had been put in an untenable position by the story in the *Daily Express*. 'If I can't trust your club to keep it quiet on the first day, then I'm not going to be able to trust them in the future,' I said. 'That's it. I'm not coming.'

He insisted that we had shaken hands. 'That's right,' I said. 'But Everton didn't fulfil its promise.' He said he didn't know how the news leaked. Little of major importance in football escapes the newspapers. Too many people know. Too many people want to boast to their friends that they know what is going on. It is hard to keep a secret, which is why managers and directors go to such lengths as meeting incognito in motorway car parks to avoid detection.

I told the Everton director to summon his hired car back to Liverpool. And I sat down and wrote a letter about why I had turned down the offer. By this time I had calmed down. I could see no reason why the day's events should sour relations between the two clubs, and in my letter I wrote: 'I am both honoured and privileged that your board considered me worthy of the task of managing such a great club and am dismayed and disappointed that I am no longer in a position to accept. If I had left, it was obvious that I was going to decimate a great deal of what I had achieved at Ipswich.

'Having literally built up the club since I joined eight years ago, I could not let this happen. I have a strong emotional tie with the club, and bearing in mind our challenge for the League Championship this season and the bright future I can foresee, the timing of your approach could not have been more unfortunate.

'I can only hope that I have not caused too much inconvenience, aggravation and confusion. I shall always take a close interest in the future of Everton and hope you get the best possible candidate to become manager.

'It is inevitable that our paths will cross, and I hope that our personal relationships will not be strained and that you will look forward to coming to Ipswich as much as I always look forward to going to Everton.' I had a letter back three days later couched in the friendliest of terms. The saga had ended fortunately without any lingering ill will.

But it left me quite drained, and I said to Elsie: 'I'll fulfil my contract. We're happy here. Money isn't everything. If I keep listening to offers it's going to be another nightmare.' So I had eighteen months of relative stability, during which time we won the FA Cup and I felt rewarded for my efforts.

In 1978, however, Barcelona made a tentative approach. They

wanted to know if I was interested in becoming their coach. We didn't get round to discussing money. I said: 'No, I'm happy where I am.' That contented state lasted until June 1979, when I was invited by Ron Greenwood to join the England summer tour of Bulgaria, Sweden and Austria. I was resting in the team's hotel in Vienna when I received a call from Edward Stirrup, a London travel agent with connections in Spain. He said Bilbao wanted me as their coach. 'When can we meet you?' he said.

'Hang on,' I said. 'Let me get home first.' Later in June I flew to Bilbao with Stirrup and met the Bilbao President, because it was an idea which had some appeal and I fancied a few days in Spain. I was offered £60,000 a year after tax, or £120,000 for two years, a salary which was considerably more than I was receiving at Ipswich.

I hoped I could keep it quiet, but knew it had to leak – and it did. Out there I met Dave Underwood, the former Fulham goalkeeper, and Ronnie Allen, who was once the Bilbao coach – they were attending a wedding – and they both advised me to stay at home. The risk of being caught up in terrorism was spelled out to me, and Allen also warned that it was a very political club.

I told Patrick Cobbold, and he said that if I went, the club would want £200,000 in compensation. Bilbao refused to pay it and the matter was dropped. I was tempted, however, because I fancied working abroad and learning another language. I thought that after two years I could come back to England a better coach, and certainly a richer one.

All my feelings about wanting to work abroad were revived in April 1980, when the football agent Dennis Roach rang and said Barcelona wanted me. I said: 'But they wanted to talk to me before and it wasn't a firm offer.'

'This time the job is yours,' he said. 'You're the one.' The previous season we had lost on away goals in Barcelona in the quarter-final of the European Cup Winners' Cup. I did not think they were a good side. With a fully fit team, Ipswich would have beaten them easily. But the stadium and the club itself were quite staggering. It was one of the world's greatest clubs, and had a stadium with a capacity of 100,000, recently increased to 130,000 in time for the World Cup.

I felt it was a good time to go there. I could learn Spanish, and when England qualified for the Finals, as I felt certain they would, I could be invaluable to Ron Greenwood. It would be the climax of my career. Not many English coaches are offered a job of this magnitude.

That Saturday Ipswich beat Coventry 3–0 and played exceptionally well – in front of a crowd of 20,000. Whatever I did at Ipswich, I knew I could never match the thrill of sending a team out in front of 130,000 fans in Spain.

I said to Patrick Cobbold in the boardroom after the match: 'You must be getting fed up with me, but I've had another offer. It's Barcelona, and I feel it's right for me.'

'If that is what you want, then okay, go and see what they say,' he replied. I said compensation would be no problem. Barcelona were one of the world's richest clubs. The following week I flew to Barcelona to talk terms with the president and vice-president. They offered me £80,000 net a year, plus £35,000 in guaranteed bonuses, and wanted to give me a two-year contract. In that time I would earn £230,000 after tax, an incredible amount by English standards. I said I wanted a three-year contract. No, they said, we never give more than two.

This time, I thought, I had to go. They even promised to pay up my contract after a year if I failed. I could walk out a failure with £115,000 in my pocket! But the president warned: 'You must win. You must get results.' It was a pressure cooker of a club, but I was confident I could stand the heat. I would be purely a coach. All the administration work I did at Ipswich would be done by other staff. I felt it was going to be a highly-paid sabbatical, and I offered to return to Ipswich after two years if they wanted me. That didn't appeal too much to Patrick Cobbold, however. 'If you go, we've got to appoint someone else,' he said.

I was conditioning myself to the prospect of working abroad. The Barcelona president said he was trying to sign Diego Maradona, the Argentine player who was the successor to Johan Cruyff as the most exciting player in world football. 'You think we ought to get him?' he asked me. 'You get him,' I said.

I rang Hennes Weisweiller, the West German coach who had worked at Barcelona, to seek his advice. 'It is a very political club,' he said. 'Your brain will go pop. The Press will be after you every minute of the day. There is hardly any reserve football, and they have twenty-four players who all want to play in the first team. You will earn much money but you will deserve every penny.'

His cautionary words did not deter me. I was determined to go there. How many coaches have the opportunity of working with Maradona? How many have a stage like the Camp Nou Stadium?

Ipswich wanted £150,000 compensation, and I thought that would present no problems to a club that was willing to pay up to three million to sign Maradona. But, to my astonishment, Barcelona refused to pay a penny in compensation. It was not their practice, they said. I was stunned. All they would offer was £35,000 for playing in their pre-season tournament the following August, a tournament which we were to play in anyway.

An agonizing few days followed. I felt the attitude of the Ipswich directors was less than fair. It was true that they had shown great loyalty to me in the early days, but I maintained that I had repaid it many times over. If I walked out of my contract with them, I might have been able to prove in a subsequent court action that they had prevented me from accepting a more remunerative job abroad. If the case had reached the courts, I suspected they would lose it. My mind was in a turmoil.

I could have flown off to Spain and left them to sue me. But once again my ties with Ipswich were too strong. When I realised that Barcelona weren't going to pay up, I accepted the inevitable conclusion. I would be staying.

The offer from Sunderland in the summer of 1981 was the most remarkable of the many I have had over the years. Tom Cowie, the Sunderland chairman, said he would pay me a starting salary of roughly twice my Ipswich salary, making me the highest paid manager in Britain.

He rang me and said: 'You can have any length of contract you like. I want you to get this show on the road. I want a team here to play some decent football and get the crowds back. My word, the public here don't half deserve it.'

Ken Knighton and Frank Clark had been sacked, and he wanted a leading manager to take over. As someone from the North-East, he knew Sunderland had a strong emotional pull for me. Some clubs, like Ipswich, have a team and a limited crowd potential. Others, like Sunderland, have no team but a great crowd. I knew that if Sunderland started winning matches Roker Park would be full again. The recession wouldn't make that much difference. Football is a religion to those people, as it is to me. They would be back.

If Ipswich hadn't won the UEFA Cup, I think I might have taken Mr Cowie's offer. But when I looked round the dressing-room in

Amsterdam I realised that I couldn't leave a club that I had built up over the years into one of the best known and most respected in Europe. I couldn't walk out on all that talent, so I turned Sunderland down. When I told Patrick Cobbold, he reacted in a typically expansive manner. He offered me a new ten-year contract. 'The only way Bobby Robson will leave this club with our blessing is to become manager of England,' he said.

Bobby Robson in the Transfer Market

In thirteen years at Ipswich Bobby Robson's record in the transfer market has been a remarkable one. He has bought just fourteen players for a mere £1,038,000 – a record unequalled in the Football League. Nearly all his players have been home produced. In that time he has sold forty-five players for £2,658,050.

So his trading in players shows a profit of £1,620,050. Again, this is a record unequalled in a League where £1m has often been spent on just *one* player.

His full transfer record is as follows:

Selling				**£**
Jan 1969	Eddie Spearritt	to:	Brighton	10,000
March 69	Ken Hancock		Tottenham	7,000
March 69	Ray Crawford		Colchester	12,500
May 69	Danny Hegan		WBA	80,000
July 69	Bill Houghton		Leicester	6,000
Nov 69	John O'Rourke		Coventry	80,000
June 70	Ron Wigg		Watford	20,000
Oct 70	Chris Barnard		Torquay	8,000
Oct 70	Bobby Hunt		Charlton	10,000
Oct 70	Steve Stacey		Bristol City	5,000
Nov 70	Chas Woods		Watford	9,000
March 71	Bill Baxter		Hull	11,250
Oct 71	Frank Brogan		Halifax	4,000
Nov 71	Tommy Carroll		Birmingham	20,000
Nov 71	Terry Shanahan		Halifax	6,000
July 72	Jimmy Robertson		Stoke City	80,000